Hymns to the Virgin and Christ,

The Parliament of Devils,

and other

Religious Poems.

Hymns to the Virgin & Christ,

The Parliament of Devils,

and other

Religious Poems,

CHIEFLY FROM

THE ARCHBISHOP OF CANTERBURY'S LAMBETH MS. No. 853.

EDITED BY

FREDERICK J. FURNIVALL,

M.A., TRIN. HALL, CAMB.; MEMBER OF COUNCIL OF THE PHILOLOGICAL
AND EARLY ENGLISH TEXT SOCIETIES.

THE EARLY ENGLISH TEXT SOCIETY

OXFORD
UNIVERSITY PRESS

Great Clarendon Street, Oxford OX2 6DP
United Kingdom

Oxford University Press is a department of the University of Oxford.
It furthers the University's objective of excellence in research, scholarship,
and education by publishing worldwide. Oxford is a registered trade mark of
Oxford University Press in the UK and in certain other countries

© The Early English Text Society 1867

The moral rights of the authors have been asserted

Database right Oxford University Press (maker)

First Edition published in 1867

All rights reserved. No part of this publication may be reproduced,
stored in a retrieval system, or transmitted, in any form or by any means,
without the prior permission in writing of Oxford University Press,
or as expressly permitted by law, or under terms agreed with the appropriate
reprographics rights organization. Enquiries concerning reproduction
outside the scope of the above should be sent to the Rights Department,
Oxford University Press, at the address above

You must not circulate this book in any other form
and you must impose this same condition on any acquirer

Published in the United States of America by Oxford University Press
198 Madison Avenue, New York, NY 10016, United States of America

British Library Cataloguing in Publication Data
Data available

Library of Congress Cataloging in Publication Data
Data available

Original Series, 24

ISBN 978-0-85-991811-4

PREFACE.

AFTER telling Mrs Gaskell one day a story for the truth of which I could not vouch, she said, with her beautiful bright smile, "Now I'm going to believe that, whether it's true or not. It ought to be true." On looking through the Lambeth MS. 853, which Mr Stubbs kindly handed to me in Lambeth Palace Library, I could not help saying, "I'll print it all, whether it contains early versions or late; it *is* a jolly little Manuscript":—a chubby vellum quarto, written in a large, clear, upright hand, which looked at first sight fourteenth century, but which the Museum authorities whom I afterwards consulted put at about 1430 A.D. As nice a little volume as one would wish to handle; a pleasing contrast to the shabby, scrubby, paper Percy folio of two hundred years later that I am now working at. Accordingly, the whole MS. is in type for the Society, and I hope members have no cause to regret it, for though earlier versions of some of the poems are no doubt in existence,—I have printed one at least sixty years older at pp. 106, 108, 110, 112, to show how the late text has changed[1]—yet the Lambeth MS. has given us the better text of *The Complaint of Christ*, in "Political, Religious, and Love Poems," (E.E.T.S., 1866,) a better text of "The Parliament of Devils" than that printed by Wynkyn de Worde, and the best texts yet printed of the far-famed *Stans Puer ad Mensam*, "How the Good Wife taught her Daughter," and "How the Wise Man taught his Son," &c.: these, besides other poems of considerable

---

[1] Two words at least of the earlier text—*sauȝten* and *vnsauȝte*, "to reconcile" and "unreconciled, at enmity," p. 108, l. 37-38, were unknown to the late scribe, and were changed by him to *soften* and *unsoft*.

beauty and interest in the present volume, and the other Texts I have lately edited, or am now editing, for the Society. The early Englishman, like the modern one, was a religious and superstitious person, and as any one in 2360 A.D. should know of us, that in many educated (or deducated[1]) persons' minds now, baptism by an episcopally-ordained clergyman is necessary to salvation, that a man's being drowned while boating on Sunday is a just judgment of God, whereas a similar death on Monday is a sad accident, with a hundred other like notions[2]; so we should know of our forefathers, if we would estimate them aright, what their religious belief and superstitious fancies were. Mary-worship, Parliament of Devils, Stations of Rome, St Gregory's Trental, and what not: let us have them all: all the nonsense, as well as the expressions of the pure, simple faith, that through life and death our men of old held to. And a survey of our early religious poetry will, I believe,—and so far as I may speak from some work at it,—result in a verdict favourable to the plain good sense

[1] We sadly want some word like this *deducate, deducation,* &c., to denote the wilful down-leading into prejudice and unreason, in Politics at least, so prevalent in England and everywhere else, to support unjust social arrangements and abuses because they exist, or are in the interest of a powerful class, &c. Let any one think of the amount of deducation attempted about the Repeal of the Corn Laws, the old and modern Reform Bills, the late American War, &c., and then see how hard the deducators still are at their work!

[2] "Dr Pusey has written another letter to the *Times,* stating his opinion of absolution. He believes that Christ, conferring upon the Apostles the power to remit sins, intended to confer it also upon their 'successors.' He therefore holds that every successor has the power to remit the sins of penitent persons as fully as Christ himself could have done; and so he affirms, on the authority of the Ordination Service, the Church of England also holds. *In other words,* Christ intended to leave the salvation of souls dependent on the will of such human beings as can be proved to have been ordained by the ordained up through the ages to Himself. One single unordained Bishop, say in the middle ages or the third century, would spoil the whole arrangement. Why does not Dr Pusey claim the power of working miracles given to the Apostles at the same time? The invisibility of the power is no greater obstacle in the one case than the other. If the sick did not get visibly better for the priest's touch, neither do the bad get visibly better for his absolution. After all, does the human race advance? A Roman gentleman would have smiled at a superstition so gross as that which Dr Pusey dignifies with the name of Christianity." 1866, Dec. 1, *The Spectator,* p. 1326, col. 1-2. Dr Pusey and his school may not admit the correctness of the statement above, "In other words." I only wish to register here the opinion of one of our best edited weeklies on this point, and to note that however comical the view stated, and a thousand like ones, may seem to our man of 2360 A.D. they were equally so to many in 1866 A.D.

PREFACE. ix

and practical going straight at the main point which Englishmen pride themselves on, whatever amount of philistinism and humbug is mixed up with these qualities. The burden of the early songs (as I read them) is a prayer for forgiveness of sins, a desire to get out of the filth of the flesh, and rise, as well here as hereafter, into the purer and higher life which, to the believer, union with his Saviour implied and implies.

Many of the poems in this volume seem to me very touching and beautiful, and I hope other readers will find them so too. The most interesting to me is the one I have entitled, from l. 638 in it, p. 78, "The Mirror of the Periods of Man's Life, or Bids of the Virtues and Vices for the Soul of Man," pp. 58-78. It sketches the temptations of the well-off man of the period—the MS. is ab. 1430 A.D.—from the time when he was new-born from his mother till, at a hundred years old, Overhope and Wanhope (despair) would ruin him, but Good Hope and Good Faith bring him to trust in God's mercy. At twenty—which may be a misprint for fifteen, xx for xv,—this is the choice presented to the young man.

> Quod resoun, " in age of .xx. ȝeer.
> Goo to oxenford, or lerne lawe."
> Quod lust, " harpe & giterne þere may y leere,
> And pickid staffe & buckelere, þere-wiþ to plaue,
> At tauerne to make wommen myrie cheere,
> And wilde felawis to-gidere drawe,
> And be to bemond[1] A good squyer
> Al nyȝt til þe day do dawe.

[1] For an explanation of this *bemond*, I have asked in vain Mr Chappell, Mr Way, Mr Morris, Mr Skeat, Mr Wright, &c., &c. The only interpretation I can suggest is drawn from a passage in Le Venery de Twety, Cotton MS. Vesp. B. xii., printed in *Reliquiæ Antiquæ*, vol. I., pp. 149-154. At pp. 152-3 we read, of the hounds hunting the hare, " And if eny fynde of hym, where he hath ben, Rycher or *Bemond*, ye shall say, *oyez a* Bemond *le vayllaunt, que quide trovere le coward, ou le court cow.*" The name *Bemond* might easily pass from the leading hound to the leader of a revel, or be used, by personification, for a fancied god of indulgence in women and wine, a sort of Bacchus. I think it certain that this *bemond* has nothing to do with the *bemol* (flat, ♭), and *bequarre* (natural, the square b, ♮) of the curious song on learning music in *Reliquiæ Antiquæ*, vol. I., p. 292, or the *bemy* of the Burlesque, p. 83, *ib.* last line. In our early music books B is *si*, though in the earliest I have seen, no name is given to it.

Conscience's remonstrance that this will waste his friends' money and his own time and learning, is answered by

"Good conscience, goo preche to þe post,
Þi councel saueriþ not my tast ...
Al my lust y wole ful-fille,
I wole spare no womman."

After the advice of Pride, Gluttony, Lechery, Wrath, Envy, Sloth, Covetousness, and Avarice, to the young man, how to indulge his passions and lusts, comes Pride again with this bit of counsel as to dress :

"Apparaile þe propirli," quod Pride,
"Loke þi pockettis passe þe lengist gise ;
Slatre þi clothis boþe schorte & side [= wide]
Passinge all oþere mennis sise."

And so the poem continues with allusions, more or less, to the manners of the times. The *pockettis* of the verses last quoted serve to fix the date of the composition of the poem, if they are (as I suppose them to be) what Camden in his Remaines, p. 196, calls "*pocketting sleeves.*"[1] He says

"Of the long pocketting sleeves in the time of King Henry the Fourth, Hocclive, a master of that age, sings,

Now hath this land little need of broomes
To sweep away the filth out of the streete,
Sen side sleeves of pennilesse groomes
Will it up licke, be it dry or weete."

The woodcut of the Duke of Gloucester[?] on p. 153 of Mr Fairholt's *Costume in England*, copied from the Royal MS. 15 E 4 (fol. 14), in the British Museum, shows the long pocket sleeve admirably, and 'his crimson jacket furred with deep red is exceedingly short,' but gathered in close folds behind. At p. 159 of Fairholt is another woodcut of an attendant with the pocket sleeve, from the same Royal MS. 14 E 4. On fol. 133 of the same Royal MS. are three figures with the long pocket sleeves, and one of them has his sleeves tied

---

[1] Pockets begin to appear in women's dresses in Edward the Third's time, says Fairholt, and are shown in that king's daughter's dress on the south side of his tomb in Westminster Abbey, as copied in Fairholt, p. 100.

behind his back, just below the bottom of his jacket. The very wide and short doublet seems not to have appeared till about 1460, and not to have been slashed. The tighter plaited jacket of Edward the Fourth's reign, also contemporary with pocket sleeves, had "large sleeves, open at the sides to display the shirt beneath," as shown in the cut on pages 154 and 159 of Fairholt. This is the only *slatring* (supposing it means *slashing*) shown in the figures, unless the opening for the arm in the long pocket sleeve be meant by the words of the poem. But the slashing of garments was at least as early as Chaucer's 'so mochil pounsyng of chiseles to make holes, so moche daggyng of sheris' (*Persones Tale*, ed. Wright, p. 143, col. 2).

The *rere* or late suppers noticed in l. 374 of this Mirror poem are complained of by Roberd of Brunne in 1303. *Handlyng Synne*, p. 226, l. 7260-3. (See also the servants' 'rere sopers' denounced, l. 7268-79.)

    Rere sopers yn pryuyte,
    Wyþ glotonye echone þey be ;
    And þyr is moche waste ynne,
    And gadryng of ouþer synne.

Doubtless Roberd was not the first preacher who inveighed against them. He also complains of the rich man lying long in bed on Sundays.

    When he heryþ a bel ryng
    To holy cherche men kallyng,
    þan may he not hys bedde lete,
    But þan behoueþ hym lygge and swete,
    And take þe mery mornyng slepe.
       Handlyng Synne, p. 135, l. 4258-62.

For the last three Poems in this volume I am indebted to Mr W. Aldis Wright, who copied them from MSS. under his charge in the Library of the Trinity College, Cambridge. The first, *Quindecim Signa ante diem Judicii*, he desired to print on account of its variations from the other earlier versions of the Poem in the E.E. Poems I edited for the Philological Society (Transactions 1858, Pt. II. pp. 7-12), in Hampole's Pricke of Conscience, the Metrical Homilies edited by Mr Small (in E. E. Poems as above, pp. 162-3), &c. The second forms a companion to the Virgin's Complaint in our *Political, Religious, and Love Poems*, 1866, and the third is given for its historic interest, and its contrast to the temper in which the later chronicler wrote of Archbishop Scrope's death.

Some of the poems bear traces of having been Southernized from a Northern original, as in using *boon* for *bane*, p. 25, l. 108, *lastande na mare*, l. 115, *siʒhande*, p. 30, l. 261, and Mr Perry has just sent me a version from the Northern Thornton MS. of the Sweetness of Jesus, pp. 8-11, here, pp. 83-6 of the Text edited by Mr Perry from the Thornton MS. that will appear with this one. I have only in conclusion to return thanks to the Archbishop of Canterbury for the loan of his pretty little Manuscript, and to Mr Aldis Wright for his help, always so willingly given, notwithstanding the pressure of crowds of other work that would overwhelm an ordinary man.

3 St George's Square, N.W.
12th November, 1866.

CORRIGENDA.

P. 27, l. 171. *Lijknes* is no doubt a miswriting of the MS. for *sijknes*, sickness.

P. 61, l. 96. *Put* " *after* dawe.

P. 119, l. 38. *For* dryve. *read* dryve, (comma for full stop).

CONTENTS.

	Page
Contents of the Lambeth MS. 853	xv-xvi
Notes	xvii-xviii

HYMNS TO THE VIRGIN.

Veni, Coronaberis	1-3
(A Song of great Sweetness from Christ to his daintiest Dam)	
Hail, Blessed Mary !	4-5
Aue Maria	6-7

POEMS TO CHRIST.

The Sweetness of Jesus	8-11
Be my Coumfort, Crist Ihesus ! . . .	12-14
Richard de Castre's Prayer to Jesus . . .	15-17
Do Merci bifore thi Iugement . . .	18-21
The Love of Jesus	22-31
Se what oure Lord suffride for oure Sake . .	32-4
I wiyte my silf myn owne Woo . . .	35-9
The Virtues of the Name Jesus (in Prose) . .	40

OTHER RELIGIOUS POEMS.

The Deuelis Perlament, or Parlamentum of Feendis .	41-57
The Mirror of the Periods of Man's Life . .	58-78
(Or Bids of the Virtues & Vices for the Soul of Man)	
God send us Paciens in oure Olde Age . .	79-82
This World is but a Vanyte (An Old Man's Lament) .	83-5
This World is false and vain	86-7

CONTENTS OF THIS VOLUME.

	Page
Earth	88-90
Reuertere (In Englisch Tunge "Turne Aȝen!") . . .	91-4
Merci passith Riȝtwisnes	95-100
(A Dialogue between a despairing Sinner and Mercy)	
The Belief	101-3
The Ten Commandments	104-5
Keep Wel Cristes Comaundement: two texts,	
I. from the Vernon MS. (Bodleian Libr.) ab. 1370 A.D.; even pages	106-112
II. from the Lambeth MS. 853 ab. 1430 A.D.; odd pages .	107-113
The Sixtene Poyntis of Charite . . .	. 114-117
Quindecim Signa ante diem Judicij . . .	118-25
Who can not wepe, com lerne of me . .	. 126-7
(The Virgin's Lament over her dead Son)	
The Death of Archbishop Scrope (8 June, 1405) .	128
Extract from Halle's *Vnion* as to Archbp. Scrope's Death .	129-30
Glossary	131-137
Notes	137
Index of First Lines	138-9

CONTENTS OF THE LAMBETH MS. 853.

	Page of MS.
1. Surge mea Sponsa (printed here p. 1-3.)	1
2. In a Tabernacle. *Quia Amore langueo.* (Political, Religious, and Love Poems, E. E. T. Soc., 1866, p. 148-50.)	4
3. In a valey (Pol., Rel., & L. Poems, 1866, p. 150-8.)	7
4. Ihesu þi swetnes (printed here p. 8-11.)	14
5. Ihesus þat sprong (here p. 12-14.)	20
6. Heil be þou Marie (here p. 4-5.)	24
7. Heil be þou Marie (here p. 6-7.)	26
8. Oratio R. de Castre (here p. 15-17.)	28
9. Whoso wilneþ. Aristotle's *A B C.* (Babees Boke, &c., E. E. T. Soc., 1867, p. 11-12.)	30
10. Whi is þis world biloued (here p. 86-7.)	32
11. Erþe out of erþe (here p. 88-90.)	35
12. In þee, god fadir. *The Belief.* (here p. 101-3.)	39
13. Man among þi myrþis. *The 16 points of Charity* (here p. 114-7.)	42
14. Every man schulde teche þis lore or *The Ten Commandments* (here p. 104-5.)	47
15. I warne eche liif or *The Ten Commandments* (here p. 107-113.)	49
16. There is no creature *Do mercy bifore þi iugement* (here p. 18-21.)	54
17. As y gan wandre or *This world is but a vanyte* (here p. 83-5.)	58
18. In a noon tijd *Reuertere* (here p. 91-4.)	61
19. Bi a forest *Right wole forþ* (here p. 95-100.)	66
20. As resoun rewlid or *Filius Regis* (Polit., Religious, and Love Poems, E. E. T. Soc., 1866, p. 205-13.)	74
21. This is goddis owne complaint (Political, Religious, and Love Poems, 1866, p. 161-9.)	81
21. If þou wole be well (Prose. Here p. 40.)	88
21. Loue is lijf (here p. 22-31.)	90

	Page of MS.		Page of MS.
22. The good wijf tauȝte hir douȝtir . . . (Babees Boke, &c., E. E. T. Soc., 1867, p. 36-47.)	102	28. Whanne Mary was greet . . *Parliament of Devils* (here p. 41-57.)	157
23. From þe tyme . *God send us paciens* (here p. 79-82.)	113	29. If so be þat lechis . (Babees Boke, &c., E. E. T. Soc., 1867, p. 54-8.)	182
24. Bothe ȝonge & olde . (here p. 32-4.)	117	30. Listniþ lordingis *How the wise man taught his Son* (Babees Boke, &c., p. 48-52.)	186
25. How Mankinde dooþ bigynne . *The Mirror* . (here p. 58-78.)	120	31. Thus oure gracious god *The Complaint of Christ* . (Political, Rel., and Love Poems, 1866, p. 169-203.)	193
26. Mi dere sone . *Stans Puer* . (Babees Boke, &c., E. E. T. Soc., 1867, p. 27-33.)	150	32. In my ȝonge age *I wiyte my silf myn owne woo* . (here p. 35-9.)	226 to 233
27. Sone y schal þee schewe *Se what Our Lord suffride* (here p. 32-4.)	155		

NOTES.

Pref. p. iv, l. 7. A just judgment of God. Compare Cotgrave's "*Vne lambe de dieu.* Soe doe the canting and blasphemous rogues of France tearme a cankered, gangrened, or desperately-sore leg. A.D. 1611.

p. 35. *I wiyte myself myn owne woo.* Sir F. Madden, in his Introduction to *Syr Gawayne*, p. lxv, notes another copy of this, "a Poem in ten eight-line stanzas, the burden of which is 'I wite my self myne owne wo,' on fol. 71 of MS. Rawlinson, C. 86, Bodleian Library. It begins 'In my youthe fulle wylde I was.'" Another is printed from MS. Cotton. Calig. A II fol. 106, v⁸ in *Reliquiæ Antiquæ,* v. 1, 197-200. It is in 15 stanzas of 8, with two introductory lines:

> I may say, and so may mo,
> I wyte mysylfe myne owene woo.

p. 41. "The *Par*lyament of Deuylles" was also "Enprynted In London In Powels chyrcheyarde By Julyan Notary. A. M. M.CCCCC. & xx"; and Wynkyn de Worde's edition of 1509 was "reprinted by Nicol for R. Heber, Esq., as his contribution to the Roxburghe Club, but for private reasons, never issued to its members." *Bohn's Lowndes.* Colophon. "Thus endeth the parlyament of deuylles. Enprynted by Wynkyn de word / prynter vnto the moost excellent pryncesse my lady the kynges moder. The yere of our lorde .M.CCCCC. & ix."

p. 58. *The Mirror.* In Admiral Swinburne's incomplete copy of *The noble lyfe & natures of man Of bestes / serpentys / fowles & fisshes y*ᵗ *be moste knowen,* by Laure*n*s A*n*drewe of ye towne of Calis, is a large cut running across both pages (a iii b, a iv), of the Ten Ages of Man, in ten double compartments, boy and man in the ten stages at top, and the ten beasts he is likened to, underneath. Below are verses applying to each age.

"Here after foloweth the ten ages of mankynde lykened be ten dyuers bestis as here is expresly shewed / and how the nature of mankynde dothe chau*n*ge from ten . . . . . tyme of a . . . . . . co . . .

> [Cut of] The .X. Ages.
>
> [Fro]M one vnto .x. a childe is he
> [Whyp]i*n*ge his toppe w*ith* sporte & playe
> [Lep]yng as ye gote right merily.
> . . . . s his care bothe nyght & day
> [At .xx. yere he is iocond an]d plesand
> . . . . t pryde
> . . . .
> . . . .
>
> ¶ At .xxx. yere he is named a man
> And syb to the bull of nature stronge
> Reue*n*ginge his right where euer he ca*n*
> with whome it be bothe short & longe

¶ Nowe forty yere he is ywys
Co*n*dicyond as a lyon in euery degre
Which maketh hy*m* often wit*h*outen mys
To lese his wysdom beleue ye me

¶ At fifty yere then can he glose
Wily as the forein worde and dede
That euer wyll wy*n*ne & neuer lose
& eke of his seruyse he wyl haue mede

¶ At threscore yere he dothe descende
But couetyse in him is roeted than
Euyn as the wolfe he doth amende*n*
ẙ woroeth the shepe wher eu*e*r he can

At .lxx. he is syb to the hownde
ẙ gnaweth ye bone so doth he his hart
All sportes he casteth to the grownde
Lest therfore his sowle sholde smart

¶ At fourscore yere withouten fayle
He is disdayned with man and wyfe
Syb to the Cat that lycketh her tayle
Euer be the fyre that is his lyfe

¶ At fourscore & x he is s . . .
Scorned of ma*n* and child h[e is]
From hym is wisdom & st[rength gone
Echone wyll his deth in b

¶ At .C. yere dethe co*m*mes . . . . . .
& maketh hi*m* as a gose y^t i[s] . . .
So plucke ye fre*n*des . . . .
But he in erthe is s . . . . . . "

p. 83. *This worlde is but a vanite.* A later copy of this Poem, with the burden "This world is but a wannyté" was printed by Mr Halliwell for the Warton Club in 1855, in *Early English Miscellanies*, p. 9-12. It has ten stanzas of eight lines each, and winds up with an extra "In Domino confydo. Amen, dico vobis."

p. 88. *Erþe vppon erþe.* In Mr Halliwell's *Early English Miscellanies* from the Porkington MS., Warton Club, 1855, is a later and somewhat different version of this poem in twelve stanzas of six, and two introductory stanzas of seven lines. Mr Halliwell calls the Porkington one "the most complete copy known to exist." It seems a late recast of the old version. Mr Halliwell also notes, p. 94, "Other versions, varying considerably from each other, are preserved in MS. Seld. sup. 53; MS. Rawl. C. 307; MS. Rawl. Poet. 32; MS. Lambeth 853 (in this text); and in the Thornton MS. in Lincoln Cathedral (fol. 279). Portions of it are occasionally found inscribed on the walls of churches."

p. 137. Note to p. 58. The inquirer as to climacterical years is referred to "A Succinct Phylosophical Declaration of the nature of clymaterical yeares occasioned by the death of Queene Elizabeth" in MS. Sloane 2117, fol. 231.

Hymns to the Virgin, Christ, &c.

Veni, Coronaberis.

(A SONG OF GREAT SWEETNESS FROM CHRIST TO HIS DAINTIEST DAM.)

(*Lambeth MS.* 853, *ab.* A.D. 1430, *page* 1.)

 SUrge mea sponsa, swete in siȝt,   *Arise, My beloved,*
  And se þi sone þou ȝafe souke so scheene; *who gavest Me suck*
 þou schalt abide with þi babe so briȝt,
4 And in my glorie be callide a queene.
 Thi mammillis, moder, ful weel y meene,   *from thy breasts;*
 Y had to my meete þat y myȝt not mys;
 Aboue alle creaturis, my moder clene,   *Above all creatures thou shalt*
8 Veni, coronaberis.   *be crowned.*

 Come, clenner þan cristal, to my cage;   *Come, My dove,*
 Columba mea, y þee calle,
 And se þi sone þat in seruage   *and see thy son who was made a*
12 For mannis soule was made a þralle.   *slave for man.*
 In þi palijs so principal
 I pleyde priuyli wiþoute mys;
 Myn hiȝ cage, moder, haue þou schal;   *Thou shalt have His high place,*
16 Veni, coronaberis.   *and be crowned.*

VENI, CORONABERIS.

Daughter of Sion, spotless flower,

thou shalt sit crowned by Me,
[Page 2.]
and all My saints shall honour thee.

F or macula, moder, was neuere in þee ;
Filia syon, þou art þe flour ;
Ful sweteli schalt þou sitte bi me,
20 And bere a crowne with me in tour,
   ¶ And alle my seintis to þin honour
Schal honoure þee, moder, in my blis,
þat blessid bodi þat bare me in bowur,
24 Veni, coronaberis.

Princess of Paradise, Mother fair,

the well of mercy in thee shall bring thy blessed body to bliss.
Come and be crowned.

T ota pulcra þou art to my plesynge,
My moder, princes of paradijs,
Of þee a watir ful well gan sprynge
28 þat schal aȝen alle my riȝtis rise ;
   ¶ þe welle of mercy in þee, moder, lijs
To bringe þi blessid bodi to blis ;
And my seintis schulen do þee seruice,
32 Veni, coronaberis.

Come, My chosen one, Maiden Queen,

dwell here with Me in bliss,

and be crowned.

V eni, electa mea, meekeli chosen,
Holi moder & maiden queene,
On sege to sitte semeli bi him an hiȝ,
36 þi sone and eek þi childe.
   ¶ Here, moder, wiþ me to dwelle,
With þi swete babe þat sittiþ in blis,
þere in ioie & blis þat schal neuere mys,
40 Veni, coronaberis.

[Page 3.]
Sweet Mother, remember the dew that dropped from our lips when we kissed.

Come and be crowned.

V eni, electa mea, my moder swete,
Whanne þou bad me, babe, be ful stille,
Ful goodli oure lippis þan gan mete,
44 With briȝt braunchis as blosmes on hille.
   ¶ Fanus distillans it wente with wille,
Oute of oure lippis whanne we dide kis,
þerfore, moder, now ful stille,
48 Veni, coronaberis.

VENI, CORONABERIS.

    Veni de libano, þou loueli in launche,   Come from Lebanon, thou
    þat lappid me loueli with liking song,   who sangst Me to sleep,
    þou schalt abide with a blessid braunche,
52   þat so semeli of þi bodi sprong.
¶ Ego, flos campi, þi flour, was solde,   Me who on Calvary cried to thee.
    þat on calueri to þee cried y-wys :
    Moder, þou woost þis is as y wolde ;
56   Veni, coronaberis.

    Pulcra vt luna, þou berist þe lamme,   Lovely as moonlight,
    As þe sunne þat schineþ clere,
    Veni in ortum meum, þou deintiest damme,   come thou to Me.
60   To smelle my spicis [1] þat here ben in fere.
    My palijs is piȝt for þi pleasure,   [Page 4.] My palace is dight with blossoms of bliss.
    Ful of briȝt braunchis & blosmes of blis ;
    Come now, moder, to þi derling dere !   Come, Mother, come and be crowned.
64   Veni, coronaberis.

    Quid est ista so vertuose   Who is she that shall endure for
    þat is euere lastyng for hir mekenes ?   ever for her meekness?
    Aurora consurgens graciouse,
68   So benigne a ladi, of such briȝtnes,
¶ þis is þe colour of kinde clennes,
    Regina celi þat neuere dide mys ;   The Queen of Heaven, who never sinned.
    þus endiþ þe song of greet sweettnes,   Come thou then, and be crowned!
72   Veni, coronaberis.

[*Quia Amore Langueo*, or "In a tabernacle of a tour," and its continuation "In a valey of þis restles mynde," printed in *Political, Religious, and Love Poems*, pp. 148-150, follow here. Then "Ihesu, þi swetnes," p. 8, and "Ihesus þat sprong, p. 12, of this volume.]

[1] Compare "Awake, O north wind, and come, thou south; blow upon my garden, *that* the spices thereof may flow out. Let my beloved come into his garden, and eat his pleasant fruits." *Solomon's Song*, ch. iv. 16. "My beloved is gone down into his garden, to the beds of spices, to feed in the gardens, and to gather lilies." vi. 2.

Hail, Blessed Mary!

[*Lambeth MS.* 853, *ab.* 1430 A.D., *page* 24.]

The heavy Clarendon letters mark the red of the MS.

<table>
<tr><td>Hail, Mary, Mother of</td><td></td><td>**H**Eil be þou, marie, þe modir of crist,
Heil þe blessidist þat euere bare child!
Heil þat conceyuedist al wiþ list</td></tr>
<tr><td>the Son of God! Maiden, never defouled,</td><td>4</td><td>þe sone of god boþe meeke & mylde!
¶ Heil maide sweete þat neuere was filid!
Heil welle and witt of al wijsdome!</td></tr>
<tr><td>fairest flower of the field.</td><td>8</td><td>Heil þou flour! heil fairest in feeld!
Aue regina celorum!</td></tr>
<tr><td>Hail, comely Queen,</td><td></td><td>**H**eil comeli queene, coumfort of care!
Heil blessid lady boþe fair & briȝt!</td></tr>
<tr><td>healer of all pain.</td><td>12</td><td>Heil þe saluour of al sore!
Heil þe laumpe of lemys liȝt!</td></tr>
<tr><td>[Page 25.] Hail, mother of Christ,</td><td></td><td>¶ Heil þou blessid beerde in whom [crist] was piȝt!
Heil ioie of man boþe al and sum!
Heil pinacle in heuene an hiȝt,</td></tr>
<tr><td>the king of Angels.</td><td>16</td><td>**Mater regis angelorum!**</td></tr>
<tr><td>Hail, fairest of all, who bred our bliss, on whom all women in child-bed call.</td><td>20</td><td>**H**eil crowned queene, fairest of alle!
Heil þat alle oure blis in bradde!
Heil þat alle wommen on doon calle
in temynge whanne þei ben hard bistadde!</td></tr>
<tr><td>All fiends dread thee, who feddest thy Son with maiden milk, Thou flower of virgins.</td><td>24</td><td>¶ Heil þou þat alle feendis dredde,
And schulen do til þe day of doome!
Wiþ maidens mylk þi sone þou fedde,
O maria, flos virginum.</td></tr>
</table>

Heil fairest þat euere god foond,
Whiche chees þee to his owne bour!
Heil þe lanterne þat is ay liȝthond!
28 To þee schulen loute boþe riche & poore.
¶ Heil spice swettist of sauour!
Heil þat al oure ioye of come!
Heil of alle wommen fruyt & flour!
32 **Velud¹ rosa vel lilium.**

Heil be þou goodli ground of grace!
Heil blessid sterre upon þe see!
Heil of coumfortis in euery caas!
36 ¶ Heil þe cheeuest of charitee!
Heil welle of witt and of merci!
Heil þat bare ihesu, goddis sone!
Heil tabernacle of þe trynyte!
40 **Funde preces ad filium.**

Heil be þou virgyne of virgins!
Heil blessid modir! heil blessid may!
Heil norische of sweete ihesus!
44 Heil cheefest of chastite, forsoþe to say!
¶ Lady, kepe vs so in oure last day
þat we may come to þi kingdom!
For me & alle cristen þou pray,
48 **Pro salute fidelium. Amen.**

Hail, choice of God,

whom rich and poor adore.

Hail, fruit and flower of womankind.
[1 P *velud; l, u,* and *d* rubbed]

Hail, Star upon the sea,

chiefest in charity,

tabernacle of the Trinity.

Hail, blessed maiden,

In our last day bring us to thy realm.

Pray for all faithful souls!

Aue Maria.

[Lambeth MS. 853, ab. 1430 A.D., fol. 26. Partly written without breaks.]

<small>Hail, Mary, Queen and Star of Heaven! help me and hear my prayer.
[¹ Page 27.]</small>

HEil be þou marie, cristis moder dere,
þat art queene of heuen, fair and sweete of chere,
þat art sterre of heuen schinynge briȝt & clere!
4   Helpe me, lady ¹ ful of myȝt, & heere my praiere
      Aue maria.

<small>To thee I make my moan: let me not die in any of the Seven Sins.</small>

Heil blessid marie, mylde queene of heuen!
Blessid be þi name, ful good it is to nempne:
8   To þee, lady, y make my moone; I praie þee
  heere my steuen,
And let me neuere die in noon of þe synnis
  seuene.
      Aue maria.

<small>Hail, Mary, flower of all!

To thee I pray!

be by me when I die,

and save me from Satan's bonds.</small>

Heil be þou marie þat art flour of alle,
12   As roose in eerbir so reed!
To þee, ladi, y clepe and calle,
To þee y make my beed;
þou be in stide & in stalle
16   Whanne y schal drawe to deed,
And lete me neuere falle
  in boondis of þe queed!
      Aue maria.

<small>Grant me my prayer,</small>

20   **H**eil be þou, marie, þat hiȝ sittist in troone!
  Y bisechе þee, swete lady, graunte me my
    boone,

Ih*esu* to loue & drede, & my lijfe to amcende soone, *amend my life,*
And bring me to þat blis þ*at* neu*er*e schal be *and bring me to everlasting bliss.*
doone.

24 **Aue maria.**

Heil be þ*o*u marie, gloriouse moder hende! *Send me meek-*
Meeknes & honeste, w*ith* abstynence, me sende, *ness and charity, that I may go to*
W*ith* chastite & charite i*nto* my lyues eende, *heaven.*
28 And þat þoru3 þi p*r*aier, lady, I mote to heue*n*
blis weende!

Aue maria.

[*Oratio Magistri Richardi de Castre*, p. 15, below, follows here.]

Poems to Christ.

The Sweetness of Jesus.

[*Lambeth MS.* 853, *ab.* 1430 A.D., *page* 14.]

<small>Jesu, beside Thy sweetness all</small>

 IHesu, þi swetnes, who-so myȝte it se,
 And þerof haue a cleere knowynge,

<small>earthly love is bitter.</small>

 Al erþeli loue bittir schulde be
4 Saue þin a-loone wi*th*out leesinge.

<small>Teach me</small>

 I praie þee, lord, þat lore leere me,
 Aftir þi loue to haue longynge,

<small>firmly to set my heart on Thee.</small>

 And sadli to sette myn herte on þee,
8 In þi loue to haue most liking.

<small>No earthly love delights like Thine,</small>

 So likinge loue in erþe noo*n* is ;
 I*n* soule who-so coude hi*m* soþeli se,
 Hi*m* to loue were mykil bliss,

<small>the King of Love.</small>

12 For king of loue callid is he.
 ¶ Wi*th* true loue, y wolde þis,
 So faste to hi*m* bou*n*de be,

<small>I would my heart were wholly Thine.</small>

 þat myne herte were holli his
16 So þat no þing likid me but he.

<small>[Page 15.]
If Nature bids me love my kin, I should love Thee first, who didst</small>

 IF y for kyndenes schulde loue my kyn,
 þan me þenkiþ in my þouȝte
 Bi kyndeli skile y schulde bigynne
20 At hi*m* þat haþ me maade of nouȝt.

<small>put Thy likeness in my soul.</small>

 ¶ His lijknes he sette my soule with-i*n*ne,
 And al þis world for me haþ wrouȝt,
 As fadir he fondid my loue to wy*n*ne,
24 For to heuene he haþ me brouȝt.

As moder of him, y make now mynde,
þat bifore my birþe to me toke hede,
And siþen with baptym waischiþ þat kynde
28 þat foulide was þoruȝ adams dede.
 ¶ With noble mete he norischiþ oure kynde,
For with his fleisch he doþ us fede,
A bettere fode may no man fynde,
32 To lastynge lijf it wole us lede.

Before my birth He cared for me, and now feeds our race with His blood.

Oure broþer & sustir he is bi skile,
For he so seide, & lerid us þat lore
þat who so wrouȝte his fadris wille
36 Briþeren & sustren to him þei wore.
 ¶ Mi kinde also he took þer-tille,
Ful truli truste y him þerfore
þat he wole neuere lete me spille,
40 But wiþ his mercy salue my sore.

He is the brother and sister of those who do His Father's will.

[Page 10.]

He took my nature, and so I trust Him.

The loue of him passiþ, certis,
Al erpeli loue þat may ben here ;
God & man, my spouse he is,
44 Weel ouȝte y, wrecche, to loue him dere.
 ¶ Boþe heuen and erþe holli is his,
He is lord of greet powere,
Callid he is þe kyng of blis,
48 His loue me longiþ for to leere.

His love passes all earthly love, and He is my spouse.

His name is King of Bliss.

Aftir his loue me þenkiþ long
For he haþ myne ful dere y-bouȝte ;
Whanne y was wente fro him with wrong,
52 From heuen to erþe he me souȝte.
 ¶ Mi wrecchid kynde for me he fonge,
And al his nobley he sette as nouȝt,
Pouert he suffride, & peynes stronge,
56 Aȝen to blis or he me brouȝte.

He bought my love full dear,

took my wretched nature, and brought me to bliss.

THE SWEETNESS OF JESUS.

[Page 17.]
Love for me brought Him to earth,
and for that He pledged His life,

Whanne y was þral, to make me fre,
Mi loue fro heuene to erþe him ledde,
My loue aloone haue wolde he,
60 For þerfore he leide his lijf to wedde.
¶ Wiþ my foo he fauȝte for me,
Woundid he was, and bittirli bledde,

and shed His precious blood.

His preciouse blood ful greet plente
64 Ful piteuousli for me was schedde.

His sides were bloody, His heart pierced with a spear.

Hise sidis bloo and blodi were
þat sumtyme were ful briȝt of blee;
His herte was persid wiþ a spere,
68 Hise ruli woundis were ruþe to se.
¶ Mi raunsum forsoþe he paied þere,

He gave His life for my guilt.

And ȝaf his lijf for gilt of me,
His deeþ schulde be to me ful dere,
72 And perse myn herte for pure pitee.

My heart should break with pity,

For pitee myn herte schulde broke on two,
To his kyndenes if y took hede;

for I was cause of all His woe.

Encheson y was of al his woo,
76 He suffride ful harde for my mis-dede.
¶ To lastyng lijf þat y schulde go,

[Page 18.]
For me He suffered death,

He suffride deeþ in his manhede;
And whanne his wille was to lyue also,

and rose again,

80 Aȝen he roos þoruȝ his godhede.

and went to heaven.

To heuen he wente with myche blis
Whanne he ouercome his bataile,
His baner ful brode displaied is

He protects me from my foes,

84 Whanne so my fo wole me assaile.
¶ Weel ouȝte y, wrecche, to ben his,
He is þat freend þat neuere wole faile;

the friend that never fails, and asks only my love again.

No þing desiriþ he þat is,
88 But true loue aȝen for his trauaile.

THE SWEETNESS OF JESUS.

    Thus wolde my spouse for me fiʒt,   *For me He was*
    And for me was woundid sore,   *wounded sore,*
    For my loue his deeþ was diʒt;   *and died.*
92 What loue myʒte he kiþe more?
¶ To ʒelde his loue haue y no myʒte   *I cannot repay*
    But loue him hertili þerfore,   *His love, but*
    And worche weel with werkis riʒt   *only obey His*
96 þat he haþ lerid me with loueli lore.   *commands.*

    Wiþ loueli lore his werkis to fille,   *[Page 19.]*
    Weel ouʒte y, wrecche, if y were kynde,   *I must alway*
    Nyʒt & day to worche his wille,   *work His will;*
100 And euere haue þat lord in mynde.
¶ But goostli foos greuen me ille,   *but my foes and*
    And my freel fleisch makiþ me blinde;   *flesh blind me.*
    þerfore his mercy y toke me tille,   *I fly to His mercy,*
104 For betere bote can y noon fynde.

    Betere bote is noon to me
    þan to his mercy truli me take   *which is my best*
    þat with his fleisch haþ made me free,   *remedy.*
108 And me, wrecche, his childe wole make.
¶ I praie þat lord for his pitee   *O Lord, forsake*
    þat he for synne me not forsake,   *me not, but give*
    But ʒeue me grace fro synne to flee,   *me grace to love*
112 And him to loue let me neuere slake.   *Thee.*

    Ihesu, for þe swetnes þat in þee is,   *For Thy*
    Haue mynde of me whan y hens wende,   *sweetness*
    With stidfast truþe my wittis þou wis,
                                         keep me from the
116 And, lord, þou scheelde me from þe feende!   *evil one!*
¶ For þi mercy forʒeue me my mys,   *[Page 20.]*
    þat wickid werk my soule neuere schende,   *For Thy mercy*
    And lede me, lord, in-to þi blis,   *lead me into bliss,*
                                         ever to dwell
120 With þee to wone withoute eende.   AMEN.   *with Thee!*

Be my Coumfort, Crist Jhesus!

[*Lambeth MS.* 853, *ab.* 1400 A.D., *page* 20.]

Jesu,	IHesus þat sprong of iesse roote,
	As us haþ prechid þi prophete,
	Flour and fruyt boþe softe and sote,
savour sweet to man's soul,	4 To mannis soule of sauour sweete ;
	Ihesu ! þou brouȝtist man to boote
	Whanne gabriel gan marie greete,
	To felle oure foomen vndir foote,
	8 In hir þou siȝ a semeli sete :
thou Virgin's son!	¶ A mayden was þi modir meete,
	Of whom þou took fleisch for us ;
Son, and Mother, comfort me!	As ȝe may boþe my balis beete,
	12 So be my coumfort, crist ihesus.
Jesu,	Ihesu, þou art wijsdom of witt
	Of þi fadir ful of myȝt !
	Mannys soule, to saue it,
to save man's soul thou wert poorly clad, put in a cradle, [Page 21.]	16 In poore aparaile þou were piȝt.
	¶ Ihesu ! þou were in cradil knyt,
	In wede wrappid boþe day & nyȝt,
born in Bethlehem.	In bethleem born, as þe gospel writt,
	20 With aungelis song and heuene liȝt.
	Barn y-born of a beerde briȝt,
By Thy kiss to Thy mother,	Ful curteis was þi comeli cus ;
	þoruȝ uertu of þat sweete siȝte,
comfort me!	24 So be my coumfort, crist ihesus.
Jesu, who wast fair when young,	Ihesu, þat were of ȝeeris ȝong,
	Fair and fresch of hide and hue,

Whanne þou were in þraldom þrong,   *when Thou wert on the Cross,*
28 And turmentid with many a iewe,
¶ Whanne blood and watir were out wrong,
For beetinge was þi bodi blewe;   *turned'st blue,*
As a clot of clay þou were for-clonge,   *and like a clod of clay wast cast in grave.*
32 So deed in prou3 þanne men þee þrewe.
¶ But grace of þi graue grew;   *But quickly Thou arose.*
þou roos up quik coumfort to us.
For hir loue þat þis councel knewe,
36 So be my coumfort, crist ihesus.   *Then comfort me.*

Ihesu, sooþfast god and man,   *[Page 22.] Jesu, God and man,*
Two kindis knyt in oon persone,
þe wondir werk þat þou bigan
þou hast fulfillid in fleisch & bone.
Out of þis world wi3tli þou wan,   *soon Thou rose from the dead to*
Liftynge up þi silf a-loone;
For my3tili þou roos, & ran
Strei3t vnto þi fadir in trone.   *Thy Father's throne.*
¶ Now dare man make no more moone;   *Man shall mourn no more,*
For man it is þou wrou3te þus,
And god wiþ man is maade at oone,
48 So be my coumfort, crist ihesus.   *so comfort me.*

¶ Ihesu crist, holi and hende,   *Jesu, Thou sentest for Thy Mother to heaven, and set her higher*
þat beerde was blessid þat bare þee,
Aftir hir whanne þou gan sende,
52 In heuene blis wiþ þee to bee.
¶ Out of þis worlde whanne sche wende,
Boþe bodi & soule were sett in see
Hi3er þan ony of aungelis kinde,   *than the angels on a throne.*
56 In troone a-fore þe trynyte.
¶ þere may þe sone his modir se   *[Page 23.]*
In heuene an hi3 to helpen us;   *Peerless Princess, pray for me! and, Jesus, comfort me!*
þou peerless princes, praie for me!
60 And be my coumfort, crist ihesus.

BE MY COUMFORT, CRIST IHESUS!

Jesus,

  Ihesu, my souereyne sauyour,
  Almyȝti god, þere ben no moo:

rule me,
  Crist, þou be my gouernour,
64 þi feiþ lete me not fallen fro.

be my food in body and soul,
 ¶ Ihesu, my ioye and my socoure!
  In my body and soule also,
  God, þou be my strengist fode,
68 And wisse þou me whan me is wo.

 ¶ Lord, þou makist freend of foo,
  Lete me not lyue in langour þus,

stay my sorrow,
  But se my sorowe, & seie now 'ho,'

and comfort me.
72 And be my coumfort, crist ihesus.

Prince of Peace, I pray Thee
  Ihesu, to þee y crie and greede;
  Prince of pees, to þee y praye;
  þou woldist bleede for mannis nede,

help me in all my fear,
76 And suffre manye a feerdful fray.

[Page 24.]
 ¶ þou me fede in al my drede
  Wiþ pacience now and ay

let me please Thee in word and deed,
  Mi lijf to lede in word & dede
80 As is moost plesaunt to þi pay,

and die well at my day.
 ¶ And to deie weel whanne it is my day.
  Ihesu, þat deied on tree for us,

Be my comfort, Christ!
  Lete me not be þe feendis pray,
84 But be my coumfort, crist ihesus! AmeN.

[The two Hymns to the Virgin, "Heil be þou, Marie," printed on pages 4-7 of this Text, follow here.]

Richard de Castre's Prayer to Jesus.

[*Lambeth MS.* 853, *ab.* 1430 A.D., *page* 28, *written without breaks.*]

Oratio magistri Richardi de castre, quam ipse posuit.

IHesu, lord, þat madist me,	Jesu,
And wiþ þi blessid blood hast bouȝt,	
Forȝeue þat y haue greued þee	forgive what I
4 With worde, with wil, And eek with þouȝt.	have grieved Thee.
¶ Ihesu, in whom in al my trust,	
þat deied upon þe roode tree,	
Withdrawe myn herte from fleischli lust,	Withdraw my heart from fleshly
8 And from al wordli vanyte !	lust.
¶ Ihesu, for þi woundis smerte	
On feet & on þin hondis two,	
Make me meeke & low of herte,	Make me meek and lowly of
12 And þee to loue as y schulde do !	heart.
¶ Ihesu, for þi bitter wounde	
þat wente to þin herte roote,	
For synne þat haþ myn herte bounde,	Thy blood must heal my guilt.
16 þi blessid bloode mote be my bote.	
¶ And ihesu crist, to þee y calle	
þat art god ful of myȝt ;	
Kepe me cleene, þat y ne falle	Keep me pure from mortal sin.
20 In deedli synne neiþer be day ne nyȝt.	

	¶ Ihesu, graunte me myne askinge,
Let me never displease Thee.	Perfite pacience in my disese,
	And neuere mote y do þat þing
24	þat schulde þee in ony wise displese.

	¶ Ihesu þat art oure heuenli king,
Grant that I and all to whom I am bound may die well. [Page 29.]	Sooþefast god, & man also,
	ȝeue me grace of good eendinge,
28	And hem þat Y am holden vnto.

	¶ Ihesu, for þe deedly teeris
Speed my prayers that I may not be condemned.	þat þou scheeddist for my gilt,
	Here & spede my praiers,
32	And spare me þat y be not spilt.

	¶ Ihesu, for them y þe biseche
Keep Thy revenging hand from those who anger Thee.	þat wraþþen þee in ony wise,
	With-holde from hem þin hond of wreche,
36	And lete hem lyue in þi seruice.

	¶ Ihesu, moost coumfort for to se
Comfort all who are full of care.	Of þi seintis euerychoone,
	Coumfort hem þat careful been,
40	And helpe hem þat ben woo bigoon.

	¶ Ihesu, keepe hem þat been goode,
Amend all who have grieved Thee.	And ameende hem þat han greued þee,
	And sende hem fruytis of erþeli fode
44	As ech man nediþ in his degree.

	¶ Ihesu, þat art with-outen lees
Stop these wars, and send us peace.	Almyȝti god in trynyte,
	Ceesse þese werris, & sende us pees
48	Wiþ lastinge loue & charitee.

	Ihesu, þat art þe goostli stoon
	Of al holi chirche in myddil erþe,

Bringe þi fooldis & flockis in oon,   Bring Thy flocks
52   And rule hem riʒtli with oon hirde.   and folds in one;

¶ Ihesu, for [1] þi blessidful blood,   [1 Page 30.]
    Bringe, if þou wolt, þo soulis to blis   and bring to bliss all who have done me good. Amen.
    For [2] whom y haue had ony good,   [2 ? for Fro]
56   And spare þat þei han do a-mys.   AMEN.

["Who-so wilneþ," printed on pp. 11-12 of *The Babees Book*,
&c., follows here, on p. 30 of the MS.]

Do Merci bifore þi Iugement.

[*Lambeth MS.* 583, *ab.* 1430 A.D., *page* 54, *written without breaks.*]

<small>Our Creator is the maker of all,</small>

    There is no creature¹ but oon,
        Maker of euery creature,
    God a-loone, & euer more oon,
4   And þre in oon alway to endure.

<small>to whom we lament</small>

    ¶ To þat lord we make oure moone
        To whom al coumfort is, & cure,

<small>how frail we are.</small>

    To þinke how freel we ben echoon.
8   In þis world is hard auenture :
    ¶ Who-so þerof is moost ensure,
        Sunnest schal he be schamed and schent.

<small>God, be merciful before thy judgment.</small>

    Or þou þe world with fier pure,
12   Do merci bifore þi iugement.

    Lord, do mercy or þat þou deeme,
        Lest þou dampne þat þou hast wrouȝt :

<small>Damn not Thine own work to please the Devil;</small>

    What ioie were it a feend to qweme,
16   To ȝeue him þat þou hast dere bouȝt.
    ¶ Out of þi siȝt if þou us fleme,

<small>banish us not from thy sight.</small>

        We ben dampned riȝt as nouȝt ;
    Þi passioun make us briȝt & schene
20   In wil, in worde, in dede & þouȝt !

¹ A later hand has written *our* over the *ure* of ' creature,' and dotted the *ure* out.

DO MERCI BIFORE THI IUGEMENT.

¶ For whi, synne haþ us þoruȝ souȝt ;
  þer-fore ameende þou oure entent
  To þe doom or we bee brouȝt ! *Amend our purposes before Thy Judgment.*
24 Do mercy bifore þi iugement.

We axe þi mercy, þou heuenli king, *[Page 55.] We ask Thy mercy.*
  For þou art lord of ech degre ;
  Of erþe þou madist oure bigynnynge, *Thou madest us of earth, and breathedst spirit in us,*
28 And aftir with spirit enspirid us free.
¶ Wiþ trees and gras þou ȝaf us growinge,
  Wiþ beestis, feelinge lijf haue we, *giving us sentient life with beasts, and knowledge with angels.*
  And with aungils we haue vndirstondinge,
32 And þerbi we schulden know þee.
  þou baddist þat alle schulde multiplie,
  But we ben fals & necligent : *We are false, but cannot hide from Thee. Have Mercy on us!*
  For we may not hide us from þin iȝe,
36 Do merci bifore þi iugement.

Þou baddist us axe merci, & we schulden haue ; *Thou baddest us ask Mercy.*
  It dooþ us coumfort on þee to calle,
  þou hast ordeined man to saue,
40 For þi merci passiþ þi werkis alle.
¶ þi herte blood for us þou ȝaue, *Thou gavest Thine heart's blood for us :*
  þou madist us free where we were þralle :
  Lete neuere þe feend oure soulis craue
44 þat waischen was in þin holi welle !
¶ Oure fleisch is freel, it makiþ us falle, *[¹ Page 56.] our flesh is frail; give us Grace and Hope ; and*
  Wiþ grace ¹ we risen & schulen repente ;
  And in hope of þee we schal : *have Mercy on us.*
48 Haue merci to-fore thi iugement.

We axe mercy bi riȝtwijsnes, *We rely on Thy promise of*
  For þi biheest is al oure riȝt,
  And of þi greet kindenes *Mercy to us. We can do nothing*
52 þou hast mercy to us bihiȝt.

2 *

of ourselves.	¶ We ne be but erþe watirlees,
	þat to springe vertu haþ no myȝt;
	þis worldis likerose bittirnes
	56 Bireueþ us discreciou*n* & oure siȝt.
The world, the flesh, and the devil fight with us.	¶ Þe feend, þe fleisch, þe worlde, wiþ us ay fiȝt;
	þus be we taken in turment;
Have Mercy before Thy Judgment.	þerfore, lord, or þi doom be diȝt,
	60 Do merci bifore þi iugement.
We have corrupted our nature with sin;	Wiþ synne we han defoulid oure kinde,
	And kinde may we not eschewe;
	To wrappe þee, god, we ben vnkinde;
we are untrue.	64 Þou kindeli king, we ben vntrewe !
	¶ Aȝens þis can no clerk skile fynde;
	Graciose god, upon us rewe;
Remember not our trespass; [Page 57.]	Take not oure trespase in to mynde,
	68 But in þi doom lete merci sue !
we cannot escape Thee.	¶ For þouȝ we wolden from þee remewe,
	In ech place þou art present;
	Or we were born, lord, þou us knewe;
Have mercy on us.	72 Do merci bifore þi iuggement.
Lord, we commit our life to Thee;	Lord ! oure soule, oure spirit, oure lijf,
	Into þin hondis, lord, we bitake;
	Out of temptacioun and strijf,
keep us night and day.	76 Lord, kepe us wheþer we slepe or wake.
Jesu, drive	¶ Ihesu, for þi woundis fyue,
	And for þi modir sake,
the devil from us when we die; let him not seize our souls.	þe feend away from us þou dryue
	80 Whanne deeþ with us maistrie schal make,
	¶ And suffre him not oure soule away to take
	For whiche on roode þou were torent;
Have Mercy before Thy Judgment.	Aȝens þi doom we tremble & quake;
	84 Do merci tofore þi iugement !
God, mingle Mercy with Justice,	God, þou deeme us riȝtwijsli,
	Medele þou merci with exccusioun,

	For we han forfetid wro*n*gfulli ;	take heed to our contrition.
88	Take hede to o*ur*e contriciou*n* !	
	¶ We ȝeelde us synful & sory	We are sinful and sorry.
	By ¹ Knowliche & confessiou*n* ;	[¹ Page 58.]
	þi passioun & þi mercy	We plead Thy sufferings :
92	We take to oure entensiou*n*.	
	¶ Bileeue is oure saluaciou*n*,	
	W*it*h keping of þi comau*n*deme*n*t.	
	God, putte þin holi passiou*n*	put them between us and Thy Judgment.
96	Bitwixe us & þi iugeme*n*t ! Amen.	

["As y gan wandre," printed below, follows here.]

The Loue of Jesus.

(Pages 90-102, written without breaks.)

<table>
<tr><td>Love in Christ is everlasting life;</td><td></td><td>Loue is lijf þat lastiþ ay
 þere it is in crist made fest,
Whanne wele ne wo it slake may,</td></tr>
<tr><td></td><td>4</td><td> as writen han men wisest.</td></tr>
<tr><td>It turns work into rest.</td><td></td><td>¶ Þe nyȝt it turneþ in-to day,
 Traueile it turneþ in to rest :
If þou wolt do as y þee say,</td></tr>
<tr><td></td><td>8</td><td> þou schalt þanne be with þe best.</td></tr>
<tr><td></td><td></td><td>¶ Loue is a þouȝt with gret desijr,
 And also of a fair loouynge ;</td></tr>
<tr><td>Love is like a fire;</td><td></td><td>Loue y likne in-to a fier</td></tr>
<tr><td></td><td>12</td><td> þat slakeen may for no þing.</td></tr>
<tr><td>It cleanses us of sin.</td><td></td><td>¶ Loue clensiþ us of oure synne,
 loue oure blis schal bringe,
Loue þe kingis herte may wynne,</td></tr>
<tr><td></td><td>16</td><td> loue of ioie euere may synge.</td></tr>
<tr><td>The help of Love reaches to heaven.</td><td></td><td>Þe socour of loue is liftid hie,
 For into heuene it ran ;
Me þenkiþ in herte þat it is sliȝe,</td></tr>
<tr><td></td><td>20</td><td> þat makiþ þe peple boþe pale & wan.</td></tr>
<tr><td>[Page 91.]</td><td></td><td>¶ Þe beed of blis it goiþ ful nyȝ,—
 I telle ȝou it as y can,—</td></tr>
<tr><td>It couples God to man.</td><td></td><td>þerof us þenkiþ þe wey to drie,</td></tr>
<tr><td></td><td>24</td><td> For euere loue coupliþ god to man.</td></tr>
</table>

THE LOVE OF JESUS.

¶ Loue is hetter þan þe cole   *Love is hotter than coal;*
    To hem þat of it is fayn & frike,
    þe flawme of loue, who myȝte it þole,
28   If it were euermore lijke :
¶ Loue us heliþ, & makiþ in qwart,   *it cheers us, and lifts us to heaven.*
    And liftiþ us up in-to heuene-riche,
    And loue rauischiþ crist in-to oure herte,
32   I woot nowhere no loue it is lijke.

¶ Leerne to loue if þou wolt lyue   *Learn to Love*
    Whanne þou schalt hens fare ;
    Al þi þouȝt to him þou ȝeue
36   þat may þee kepe from care ;
¶ Loke þou þin herte fro him not twynne   *God, and put not thine heart from Him.*
    þouȝ þou wandre euery where,
    So þou may weelde him with-inne,
40   And loue him hertili euermore.

Ihesu, þat me loue hast lende,   *[Page 92.] Jesu! bring me to Thy Love*
    In-to þi loue þou me bringe,
    Take to þee al myn entente
44   þat þou be to me myn ȝerninge,
¶ And þat synne from me awei were went,   *that sin may leave me,*
    And loue come myn owne coueitynge,
    þat my soule hadde herd & hent   *and my soul may hear the song of Thy loving.*
48   þe songe of þi sweete louynge.

¶ þi loue is to us euerelastynge   *Thy Love lasts ever.*
    Fro þat tyme þat we may it verrili fele,
    þerinne make we euere brennynge,
52   þat no þing may it uerrili keele.
¶ Mi þouȝt, take it into þin hand,   *Take my desire to Thee*
    And stable þou it ilke a dele,
    þat y be no þing hildande   *that I may not love the world.*
56   To loue uerrili þe worldis wele.

THE LOVE OF JESUS.

If I love any earthly thing,

¶ If y loue ony erþeli þing
  þat paieþ to my wille,
And sette my ioie in foule likinge,
60 Whanne it may come me tylle

[Page 93.] at my death it will be poison

I may drede at my departynge
  þat it wole be attir & ille,
For alle my welþis ben wepinge

in hell.

64 whanne peyne my soule wolde spille.

Earthly joy,

¶ Þe ioie þat men heere seen
  Is ful likinge vnto þe iȝee;

now fresh and green, soon fades.

þat now is fair, freische, and grene,
68 And anoon aftir is welkid awey:

Such is the world;

¶ Þis is þe world, alle men moun seen,
  And wole be vnto domysday,

toil and trouble.

Ful greet traueile, & myche tene;
72 To flee þat is ful hard in fay.

If you leave evil,

¶ If þou leue yuel in al þi þouȝt,
  And hate þe filthe of synne,

and give yourself to Christ,

And ȝeue to him þat þee dere bouȝt,
76 þat he weelde þee with-inne,
¶ Al þi soule þi lord haþ souȝt,
  And þerof he wolde not mynne;

He will bring you to bliss.

þus schalt þou to blis be brouȝt,
80 And wonye heuene wiþ-ynne.

[¹ Page 94.] Love is trusty and true,

¶ For-¹soþe þe kinde of loue is þis,—
  þere it is trusty and trewe,—
To stoonde euere in stabilnes,

never changing.

84 And chaunge neuere for no newe.

He who finds it

¶ Þat wiȝt þat þat loue may finde,
  Or euere in herte it knewe,

need not care.

Fro care it turneþ þat kinde:
88 Such a mirþe fyndiþ to fewe.

THE LOVE OF JESUS.

¶ For-þi, loue þou as y þee rede ;
 Crist is trewe loue, as y þe telle ;   *Christ is true Love.*
 Wiþ auͫgilis take þou þi stide ;
92 þat ioie loke þou not felle.
¶ In erþe hate[1] þou no manͤr qweed, *[1 ? loue]*
 But loke þat þi loue may dwelle, *Let thy Love be His.*
 For loue is more strenger þan deed, *It is stronger than death and hell.*
96 Loue is more harder þan helle.

¶ Loue is liȝt, & a birþun fyne ; *Love gladdens young and old.*
 Loue gladiþ boþe ȝonge and oolde ;
 Loue is wiþout ony pyne,
100 As louͤrs han me toolde.
¶ Loue is goostli deli-²ciouse as wijn *[2 Page 95.]*
 þat makiþ meͫ boþe big & bolde ; *It is delicious as wine.*
 To þat loue y schal me so faste tyne, *Hold fast to it.*
104 þat y in herte it euͤrmore holde.

¶ Loue is þe swettiste þing *Love is*
 þat heere in erþe men may han ;
 Loue is goddis owne derlinge ; *God's own darling.*
108 Loue byndiþ boþe blood & baan.
¶ In loue, þerfore, be ouͤre likinge ; *Let our delight be in it.*
 I knowe no betere won ;
 For me oonli, & my louynge,
112 Loue makiþ boþe but oon.

¶ But al fleischli loue schal fare *Fleshly love is like May flowers,*
 As dooþ þe flouris of may,
 And schal be lastande na mare *lasting only an hour.*
116 But as it were an houͤr of a day ;
¶ And sorewen aftir þat ful sare *And after comes sore sorrow*
 Hir lust, her pride, & al her play,
 Whaͫne þei aren cast in care,
120 In-to pyne þat lastiþ ay. *in hell.*

THE LOVE OF JESUS.

[Page 96.]
When men rise again,

¶ Whanne her bodies in þe fen liggen,
  Þanne schulen her soulis be in drede,
 And up aȝen as men schulen risen,
124 And answere for her mys dede.

if they have sinned here,

¶ If þei be seen þan in synne,
  And now heere þer liif þei ledde,

they shall lie in hell.

 Þan schulen þei ligge helle wiþ-inne,
128 And derkenes haue to mede.

Rich men shall rue their sin in hell.

¶ Riche men her hondis schal wrynge,
  And her wickid werkes abie
 In flawmes of fier bitterli brennynge,
132 Wiþ care and sorewe schamefastli.

But Love, and then you'll sing to Christ.

¶ If þou wolt loue, þan may þou synge
  To þi lord crist in melodie :
 Þe loue of him ouercomeþ al þing ;
136 In loue lyue we & die.

Jesu, Son of God!

Ihesu ! god-is sone þou art,
  lord of moost hiȝ magiste,
 Sende verrili loue in-to myn herte

send Love into my heart!
[¹ Page 97.]

140 Oonly ¹ to coueite þee !
¶ Reue me likinge of þis world,

Be my Love!

  Mi loue þat þou may be ;
 Take myn herte in-to þi ward,
144 And sette þou me in stabilte !

Jesu, maiden's Son!

¶ Ihesu ! þou, þe maidens sone,
  þat with þi blood me bouȝte,

Pierce my soul with thy spear.

 Þirle my soule with þi spere anoon,
148 Þat myche loue in men hast wrouȝt.
¶ Me longiþ þou lede me into þi siȝt,
  And fastne þere in þee my þouȝt ;

Make my heart light in Thy sweetness.

 In þi swetnes make myn herte liȝt,
152 Þat al my woo wexe to nouȝt.

THE LOVE OF JESUS.

¶ I̲h̲e̲su, my god & my loueli king !
   Forsake þou not my desijr ;
   Mi þouȝt make to be meekinge ;
156   I hate boþe pride & ire.
¶ Þi wil is al my desirynge ;
   Of loue kyndele þou þe fier,
   Þat y with þi sweete louynge
160   Wiþ aungils take myn hire.

¶ Wounde þou myn herte wiþ-inne,
   And weelde me at þi wille ;
   Of blis þat neuere schal blynne,
164   Þou fastne me þat y not spille.
¶ Þat y þi loue may wynne,
   Of grace my þouȝt þou fille,
   And make me cleene of synne
168   Þat y may come þee tille.

¶ Ihesu ! putte in-to myn herte
   Þe memorie of þi pyne !
   In lijknes, and eek in qwarte,
172   Þi loue be cuere myne !
   Mi ioie is al of þee ;
   My soule, take it as þine ;
   Mi loue cuere wexinge be,
176   So þat y neuere dwynne.

¶ My loue is euere in siȝinge
   While y dwelle in þis way ;
   Mi loue is in þee longynge,
180   Þat bindiþ me niȝt & day
¶ Tille y come vnto my king,
   Þere y wone with him may,
   And se his fair schynynge
184   In lijf þat lastiþ ay.

Jesu, my God !

make me meek ;

kindle within me
the fire of Love !

Wield me at Thy
will

[Page 98.]
that I may win
Thy love

and come to Thee.

Jesu, remind me
of Thy sufferings,

give me Thy
Love,

take my soul as
Thine.

My Love sighs

and longs

till I come to my
King

in Life that lasteth
aye.

THE LOVE OF JESUS.

<ul style="list-style:none">
<li>¶ Longinge is in me so lent</li>
<li>For loue, þat y ne can lete;</li>
<li>His loue he haþ me now sent — Christ has sent me His Love.</li>
<li>188 þat euery bale may bete;</li>
<li>¶ Siþen þat myn herte was brent</li>
<li>In cristis loue so sweete,</li>
<li>Al woo fro me awei is went — All woe has left me.</li>
<li>192 And we neuere aȝen schulen mete.</li>
</ul>

<ul style="list-style:none">
<li>¶ I sitte and synge of loue longynge — I sit and sing.</li>
<li>þat in my ¹ brest is now bred.   [¹ Page 99.]</li>
<li>Ihesu, my king and my ioiynge! — Jesu, my joy,</li>
<li>196 Whi ne were y to þee led?</li>
<li>¶ Ful weel y woot in al my ȝernynge,</li>
<li>In al ioie, y schulde be fed.</li>
<li>Ihesu! me brynge to þi woninge, — bring me to Thy dwelling.</li>
<li>200 For þe blood þat þou hast bleed.</li>
</ul>

<ul style="list-style:none">
<li>¶ Demed he was on a crosse to heng, — Jesus was hung on the Cross,</li>
<li>þe fair aungelis foode;</li>
<li>Wiþ scourgis þei gan him sore swing — scourged,</li>
<li>204 Whanne þat he bounden stoode;</li>
<li>¶ His brist was bloo in betyng,</li>
<li>Not spilt was his blood;</li>
<li>þe þorn crowned þat king — and crowned with thorns.</li>
<li>208 þat doon was on þe roode.</li>
</ul>

<ul style="list-style:none">
<li>White was his nakid breest, — White was His breast,</li>
<li>& reed his bloodi side,   [See Political R. and L. Poems, p. 214.]</li>
<li>Wan was his face fairest, — wan his face,</li>
<li>212 Hise woundis depe & wide.</li>
<li>¶ þe iewis wolde not þan reste</li>
<li>To pyne him more in þat tide;</li>
<li>Al he suffride þat was wisest, — down his blood did glide,</li>
<li>216 His blood to lete doun glide.</li>
</ul>

THE LOVE OF JESUS.

¶ Blyndid were hise faire ȝen,
  And al his fleisch bloodi for-bete;   out he let his
  Hise ¹ louesum lijf þat alle men siȝe[n],   [¹ Page 100.]
220 Ful myldeli he out gan lete.   lovesome life.

¶ Deed & lijf bigunne to striuen   Life was slain,
  Wheþer myȝt be maister þere;
  Liif was slayn, & roos a-ȝen;   but rose again to give us bliss.
224 In-to blis ful fair may we fare.
¶ He þat þee bouȝt haue al þi þouȝt,
  And lede he it in to his loore;
  Ȝeue al þin herte to crist in qwarte,   Give thy heart to Christ!
228 And so to loue him euermore.

¶ I siȝe, y sobbe, boþe day & nyȝt,   I sigh and sob for Him;
  For oon þat is so fair of hue;
  þere is no þing myn herte may liȝt   nothing but He can comfort me.
232 But his loue þat is so true.
¶ Who so hadde him in his siȝte,   He alone can
  Or in his herte him knewe,
  His moornynge schulde turne into ioie briȝt,   turn mourning into joy.
236 His longynge into glewe.

¶ In mirþe lyueþ he nyȝt & day   He who loves Jesus,
  þat loueþ þat sweete childe;
  Wraþþe wolde from him awey,
240 Were he neuere so wielde.
¶ It is ihesu, forsoþe to say,   [Page 101.]
  Of alle meekist & myelde;   meekest and mildest of all,
  He þat in herte him loueþ þat day,   will be shielded from evil.
244 From yuel he wole him schielde.

¶ Of ihesu þanne moost list me speke,   Of Jesus I must speak,
  þat may of al my bale be bote;
  Me þinkeþ myn herte wole al to-breke
248 Whanne y þinke on þat soote.

THE LOVE OF JESUS.

for He has caught my heart in Love.

¶ In loue lauȝt he haþ my þouȝt,
  þat y schal neuere for-lete ;
 Ful dere me þinkeþ he haþ me bouȝt,
252 Wiþ bloodi heed, hondis, & feete.

For Love my heart will burst when I see Christ.

¶ For loue myn herte wole to-berste
  Whanne y þat fair loue biholde ;
 Loue is ful fair þere it is fest,
256 þat neuere wole be coolde.

¶ Loue us reueþ þe nyȝtis rest ;
  In grace it makiþ us boolde ;

Love is the best of all works.

 Of alle werkis loue is þe beeste,
260 As holi men me haþ tolde.

I sigh when I think on Jesus

¶ No wondir if y siȝhande be,
  And siþen in woo al bi-sett ;

nailed on the Cross,

 Ihesu was nailid upon þe tree ;
264 Ȝhe, al bloody for-beet.

¶ To þinke on him is greet pitee,
  To se how tenderli he gret ;

[Page 102.]

 þis haþ he suffride, man, for þee,

suffering for man.

268 If þat þou wolt þi synnes leett.

The sweetness of Christ's Love none can tell.

¶ þere is no lijf in erþe may telle
  Of þis loue þe swetnes :
 þat stidefastli in loue can dwelle,
272 His ioie is euere eendelees.

God keep him who Loves, from hell.

¶ God schielde þat he schulde to helle,
  þat of loue longinge kan not ceesse,
 Or euere hise enemyes schulde him qwelle,
276 Or þat he so his loue schulde lese.

Jesus is the Love that lasteth aye.

¶ Ihesu is þe loue þat lastiþ ay ,
  To him is oure longinge.
 Ihesu þe nyȝt turneþ to day,
280 And derknes in-to day spryng.

¶ Ih*e*su! þinke on us now and ay,   Jesu, think on us,
    For þee we holde oure kyng!
  Ih*e*su, ȝeue us grace þat weel may,   and give us Grace to love
284   To loue þe w*ith* oute eendynge!—A-M-E-N.   thee ever. Amen.

["The good wijf," printed in *The Babees Boke, &c.*, follows.]

Se what oure Lord Suffride for oure Sake.

[Pages 117—120, written without breaks.]

<small>Make good cheer in Christ's name.</small>

BOthe ʒonge & oolde, wheþir ʒe be,
　　in cristis name good cheer ʒe make,
and liftiþ up ʒoure hertis, & se

<small>See what he suffered for our sake.</small>

4　What oure lord suffride for oure sake.
as meeke as ony lombe was he,

<small>Like Him let us suffer too.</small>

　　ensaumple of him weel mowe we take,
& to suffre also in oure degre,
8　& in his seruice euere to wake.

<small>If friends forsake us, let us think</small>

And if oure freendis forsake us heere
　　so þat we be left al aloone,

<small>on Jesus,</small>

þinke on ihesus þat bouʒt us dere,
12　& to him make we al oure moone;
¶ For of þat lord weel may we leere
　　What wrong he suffride among hise foon;

<small>how all his disciples fled but Mary and John.</small>

Whanne hise disciplis fledden for feer,
16　þer bood no mo but marie & iohne.

<small>If wrong be wrought us,</small>

If ony wrong to us be wrouʒt,
　　Be it in word eiþer in dede,

<small>God may help at need; think how [Page 118.] Christ has bought us with His blood.</small>

Be of good hope ʒit in þi þouʒt
20　How god may us helpe alle at neede,
And þinke we how ihesus crist us bouʒt,
　　& for oure synnis hise blood wolde blede;
for his owne gilt was it nouʒt,
24　for he dide neuere synful dede.

SE WHAT OURE LORD SUFFRIDE FOR OURE SAKE.

 ¶ If wickid men do us defame,   *If men defame us,*
  þinke how crist was bouȝt & solde;
  to suffre for him is no schame,   *let us suffer for Christ,*
28 but him to serue loke we be boold.
  And if men hurte us in oure name,
   We must forȝeue, boþe ȝonge & olde,   *and forgive.*
  For þouȝ we suffre myche blame,   *He suffered 1000 fold more.*
32 crist suffride moore a þousand foold.

  And of pouert þouȝ we wolde playne,   *If poverty pinch us,*
   for þat we wanten worldli good,
  þinke we on ihesu, þat lord souereyn,   *think how Jesus hung, poor, on the Cross,*
36 how pore he heng upon þe roode,
 ¶ And how he stryued not ageyn,
  but euere was meeke & mylde of mood.   *meek and mild.*
  to folewe þat lord we schulden be fayn,   *Follow Him.*
40 in what degre þat euere we stood.

  & þouȝ we haue sorowe on ech side,   *If sorrow come, and wrong,*
   & al aboute wrong & woo,
  ȝit suffre meekeli, & a-bide,   *still suffer meekly and think on Jesus*
44 And þinke on ihesu þat suffride also,   [Page 119.]
  and how he was in ful greet drede,
   Vnto hise peynis whanne he schulde go;
  he suffride moore in hise manhede   *who suffered more than any man.*
48 þan euere dide man, or euere schal do.

 ¶ þouȝ we with wrong to deeþ be brouȝt,   *If we be wrongly brought to death,*
   ȝit suffraunce is a sikir way
  For þe loue of ihesu þat us dere bouȝt   *yet suffer still*
52 & deide for us on good friday;
  Wherfore us þinkiþ in oure þouȝt
   þat we oure lord schulde please & pay,   *and please our Lord.*
  And we to sette þis world at nouȝt,
56 And suffre we wickid men to say.

  In ihesu crist was meekenes moost,   *Christ, through meekness, overcame*
   And þerfore he þe maistrie hadde,

and bound the Devil,		*And* boond þe feend for al his boost
	60	þat he w*as* neue*re* so sore adradde.
		¶ Al aȝens his wil & al his oost
and brought Adam, Eve, and others, from hell.		Adam & eue w*ith* him he ladde,
		And many moo out of þat coost
	64	þat weren in p*ri*sou*n* ful hard bistadde.
If you follow Jesus,		*And* if þou i*n* ihe*s*u haue delite,
		þouȝ al þe world do þee assaile,
[¹ Page 120.] you shall find that Meekness will prevail,		Do aftir þis, & þou schalt wite
	68	þat meekenes ¹ Wole þee moost availe ;
		For who þat suffriþ heere dispite,
		And meekeli a-bidiþ i*n* þat bataile,
bringing you to endless joy.		it wole turne hem to greet profite
	72	& eendlees ioie for her trauaile.
If any man do you wrong,		¶ If ony man do to us a mys,
		Or wole in ony wise to us offende,
for Jesus' love		for þe loue of ihe*s*u haue my*n*de on þis,
	76	& lete meekenes þi mood ameende
		wiþ ihe*s*u c*ri*st, as oon of his,
suffer.it ; you shall dwell with Him in bliss.		*And* suffre meekeli what god wole sende,
		þa*n*ne schal we be w*ith* him in blis
	80	þ*at* eue*re* schal laste wiþoute*n* eende. A-M-E-N.

[" How mankinde dooþ bigynne," pp. 58-78 of this Text, follows here.]

J wiyte my silf myn owne Woo.

[*Lambeth MS.* 853, *ab.* 1430 A.D., *page* 226-33.]

  IN my ȝonge age ful wielde y was,   In my youth I
  Mi silf þat tyme cowde y not knowe,   was very wild,
  Y wolde haue my wil in euery place,
4 And þat haþ now brouȝt me ful lowe.   and that has brought me low,
  Þinke, ihesu, how y am þin owe !   But, Jesu, think
  For me weere þi sidis boþe pale & bloo !   how I am thine.
  To chastise me þou doist it, y trowe ;
            I blame myself
8 Y wiyte my silf myne owne woo !   for my woe.

¶ I made couenaunt, true to be,   I kept not my
  Firste whanne y baptisid was ;   baptismal covenant,
  Y took to þe world, & wente from þee,
12 Y folewide þe feend al in his traas ;   but followed the devil,
  From wraþþe and enuye wolde y not pas ;
  Coueitise and auarise y usid also,
  Mi fleische hadde his wille, alas !   let my flesh have its will,
16 Y wiyte my silf myn owne woo !

¶ Now y woot y was ful wielde,
  In þat my wil passid my witt ;
  Y was ful sturdy, & þou ful myelde ;   and was rebellious.
20 Ihesu, lord, y knowe weel it.   But, Jesu,
  Of þi blis y were ful qwytt   [Page 227.]
  If y hadde aftir þat y haue do ;
  But to þi merci y truste ȝitt,   I trust to Thy
24 Y wiyte my silf myn owne woo !   mercy.

3 *

I was proud and extravagant,	¶	I was hiʒ of herte and stowte,
		And in my cloþing wondre gay ;
		I lokide men schulde vn-to me lowte
	28	Where-so þat y wente bi þe wey.
caring only for women and dress.		Faire wommen, and good aray,
		Al myn entent y took þer-to ;
		Aʒen þi techinge euere y seide nay ;
	32	I wite my silf myn owne woo !
I trusted riches, not God,	¶	I trustide.more to worldli good
		·þan to god þat it me sente ;
		Weelþe made me hiʒ of mood ;
	36	Lust and likyng me ouer wente.
and stuck at nothing to get money.		To gete good y wolde not stente,
		Y ne rouʒte how y come þer-to ;
		To þe poore y neiþer ʒaf ne lente ;
	40	Y wiyte my silf myn owne woo !
[Page 228.] Lord, I feared Thee not,	¶	Lord, y hadde no drede of þee ;
		Mi grace wente away þerfore ;
but Thou		But, lord, as þou bouʒtist me,
	44	So lete me neuere be for-lore.
suffered'st for me.		For me þou suffredist peines sore ;
		þou art my freend, and y þi foo ;
Have mercy on me!		Mercy, lord ! y wole no more ;
	48	Y wiyte my silf myn owne wo !
Three evil things ruin a man.	¶	þer ben .iij. poyntis of myscheef
		þat ben confusioun to many a man,
		Which þat worchen to her soulis greet greef ;
	52	Y schal hem rehersen as y can.
I. The desire of poor men to look like rich ones.		Poore men proud, þat litil han,
		þei wolen be a-raied as riche men goo ;
		þei hindren hem silf & oþir þan,
	56	And mowe wiyte hem silf her owne woo.
II. The covetousness of rich men,	¶	A riche man, þeef, is anothir,
		þat of coueitise wole not slake ;

If he wi*th* wrong bigile his broþir,   *cheating others,*
60 Heuene blis he schal forsake;
   Bifore god, for þeefte it is take,   *[Page 229.]*
   Al þat wi*th* wrong he wynneþ so;   *which with God is theft.*
   But if he here a-meendis make [1]   [1 MS. *made*]
64 he schal wiyte hi*m* silf his owne woo.

¶ An oolde man lecchou*r*, þe þridde it is,   *III. The lechery*
   For his complexiou*n* wexiþ coolde;   *of old men.*
   It bringeþ þe soule to peyne fro*m* blis,
68 It stinckeþ on god so manye foolde.
   Theise .iij. þat y haue of toold   *These three please*
   Ben pleasinge to þe feend oure foo;   *the Devil.*
   Hem to use, who is so boold,
72 May wiyte hi*m* silf his owne woo.

¶ Manye defautis god may fynde   *God shows us*
   In vs þat schulde hise seruau*n*tis be;
   He schewi*th* us loue, & we vnkinde,   *love, and we look*
76 Certis þe more to blame be wee.
   Su*m*me staren broode & mou*n* not se,   *away from Him*
   Synne is þe cause it fariþ soo;   *through sin.*
   Suche dreden not god, y seie to þee,   *We may blame*
80 And may wiyte he*m* silf her owne woo.   *ourselves for our own woe.*

¶ In iij. þingis y dare weel sayn   *[Page 230.]*
   god schulde be worschipide ou*er* al þing;   *In three things we should worship God,*
   do riȝtwijsnes wi*th* m*er*ci wi*th* al þi mayn;   *Righteousness, Mercy,*
84 þe þridde is cleennesse in lyuynge: *Chastity,*
   To bischopis & curatis þat han kepi*n*ge,   *which bishops,*
   it is her charge, & to lordis also.   *curates, and lords*
   and if þei contrarie god-is biddinge,   *are bound to keep.*
88 þei may wiyte he*m* silf her owne woo.

¶ wro*n*g is an hiȝ seete þ*er*e riȝt schulde be,   *Wrong is now set*
   merci for mys deede is putt away;   *up where Right should be.*

Lechery drives away Purity.		letcherie haþ made clennesse to flee,
	92	Loue may not abide nyght ne day.
		Þus þe feend, y dare weel say,
Man, amend, or blame yourself for your own torment.		wole make oure freend oure moost foo :
		man, amende þee whilis þou may,
	96	Or wiyte þi silf þin owne woo.
I must be troubled while I follow my own will.		¶ It is no wondir þouȝ y be woo
		myn owne wil while y wole sewe,
		& my lordis bidding wole not doo :
	100	y am ful fals, but he is trewe,
[Page 231.]		And ȝit he fyndiþ me with al þing newe,
I serve the devil.		And y serue þe feend, and go him froo ;
		But if y amende, it schal me rewe,
	104	And may wiyte my silf myn owne woo.
		¶ In þre degrees þe world kept is,
Priests, knights, and labourers shall all suffer if they do wrong,		With preestis, knyȝtis, and laborere,
		And which of hem þat doon amys,
	108	þei schulen it abie wondir deer.
		Bi good ensaumplis þe preestis schuld lere
		þe vnleerned how þei schulden doo :
and blame themselves for their distress.		If her word & werk coorde not in fere,
	112	þei mowe wite hem silf her owne woo.
Lords should		¶ Knyȝthode also, lordis, ne oþir,
		Schulden not be of conscience light,
help the poor,		þei schulden helpe her poore suster or broþer,
	116	And also strengþe hem in her ryght
but instead often oppress them, and when in woe will have to blame themselves.		þoruȝ pride & coueitise summe leesen her myȝt ;
		For letcherie, grace is kept hem froo ;
		If þei biholde her owne in-syght,
	120	þei mowe wiyte hem silf her owne woo.
[Page 232.] Labourers should		¶ Þe laborer schulde truly traueile þan,
		And be riȝtful boþe in worde & deede,

I WITE MY SILF MYN OWNE WOO.

  And what-euere werkis þat he can,
124 And resonabli to take his meede.
  Wrongfulli summe her lijf heere lede,
  Among leerned & lewde it is founde so,
  And in her laste eende it is to drede
128 þei mowe wiyte hem silf her owne wo.

work well, and take reasonable wages. But some do wrong,

and will have to blame themselves.

  ¶ Man, take hede what þou art :
  But wormes meete ! þou woost weel þis ;
  Whanne þat þe erþe haþ take his part,
132 Heuene and helle schal haue his.
  If þou doist weel, þou goist to blis ;
  If þou do yuel, þou goost to þi foo ;
  Loue þi lord god, & þinke on þis,
136 Or þou wite þi silf þin owne woo.

Man, worms' food, thou must go

to bliss or hell.

Do not have to blame thyself for thy woe.

  ¶ Now ihesu crist, oure sauyour :
  From oure foos þou vs defende ;
  In al oure nede be oure socour,
140 Heere & whanne we hens wende,
  And sende us grace so to amende,
  His blisse þat we may come vnto,
  Heere to make so good an eende
144 þat wee not cause oure owne woo.
    Deo gracias.

Christ, defend us,

here and hereafter.

[Page 233.]

Bring us to Thy bliss that we may not cause our own woe.

[End of the MS. In a later hand is "This is sir Hary myndes booke, Record of John Dauis, & of sir John George & of Sir Robert george fines (?)]

The Virtues of the Name Jesus.

[Page 88.]

This name, Jesus,

when thou speakest it, it shall be honey in thy mouth and melody in thine heart.

[2 Page 89.]

Think on Jesus;

It drives out the devil, and opens heaven.

Also hail Mary often.

Keep Love in thine heart, for Love is the fulfilling of the Law.

IF þou wole be weel wit*h* god, *And* haue grace to reule þi lijf, *And* come to þe ioie of loue, þis name ihesu, fastne it so fast in þin herte þat it come neuere
4 out of þi þou;t. And whanne þou spekist to him, & seist ihesu þoruȝ custum, It schal be i*n* þin eere ioie, *And* in þi mouþ hony, *And* in þin herte melodie, For þou schalt þinke ioie to heere þe name of
8 ihesu be nempned *,[2] swetnes to speke it, Myirþe & song to þinke on it. If þou þinke on ihesu contynueli, And holde it stabli, It purgiþ þi sy*n*ne, it kyndeliþ þin herte, It clarifieþ þi soule, It remeueþ
12 anger, it doiþ a-way slownes, It wyndiþ i*n* loue fulfillid of charite, It chasiþ þe deuel, it puttiþ out drede, It openeþ heuene, it makiþ contemplatijf men haue in mynde ofte ihesu, For alle vicis &
16 fantu*m*s it puttiþ fro þe louer. Also þe*r*to heile ofte marie boþe day & nyȝt, *And* þanne myche ioie & loue schalt þou fele. And þou do aftir þis lore, þe nediþ not greetli coueite many bookis. Holde loue
20 i*n* herte & i*n* werk, *And* þou hast al þat we may seie or write, For fulnes of lawe is charite: In þat hongiþ al.

---

* There is a curl of contraction as for *er* over the second *e*.

A Song Called
Þe Deuelis Perlament,
or
Parlamentum of Feendis.

(Lambeth MS. 853, ab. 1430 A.D., Pages 157—182.)

<table>
<tr><td>

Whanne marye was greet wit<i>h</i> gabr<i>i</i>el,
    And had co<i>n</i>ceyued & bore<i>n</i> a childe,
    Alle þe deuelis of þe eir, of erþe, & of helle,
4 helden þer paralament of þat maide mylde,
¶ What man had made her wombe to swelle.
    " To tempten hir ȝe tenden to seelde ;
    her childis fadir who can telle,
8 Who dide wit<i>h</i> hir þo werkis wielde? "

¶ In helle þe feendis þoo answeride,
    " We knew neue<i>r</i>e fadir þat he hadde,
    But amongis p<i>r</i>ophetis we haue leerid
12 þat god wit<i>h</i> man haþ couenau<i>n</i>t maade :
¶ A serpent i<i>n</i> deseert was rerid,
    So schal god-is sone in man be had,
    þe soule of hi<i>m</i> schal be vnsperid,
16 his herte to-cloue, and he for-bleed.

¶ þese p<i>r</i>ophetis speken so in myst,
    What þei mente we neue<i>r</i>e knewe ;
    þei spoken of oon schulde hote c<i>r</i>ist,
20 But maries sone hiȝte ihesu ;

</td><td>

When Mary had given birth to Jesus, all the Devils held a consultation as to who had begotten Him.

The Hell-Devils did not know, but had learnt from Prophets

that God's Son was to be raised in man, and to suffer death ;

[Page 158.]
and that one, Christ, should come ; but Mary's Son was Jesus.

</td></tr>
</table>

Also that Christ should be one with God; but Jesus was not. So the Devils were puzzled.

¶ And þei seiden þat crist with god schulde be
    a-twist,
  But þis ihesu neuere in þe godhede grew;
  We ben bigilid alle wiþ oure lyst.
24 þe clooþ is al of anothir hew;

But they agreed that if God sent His Son into man's body,

¶ And þou3 god make hise perlament
  Of pees, mercy, trouthe, & resoun,
  And from heuen til erþe his sone be sent
28 In mankinde to take a cesoun,
  ¶ We schulen ordeyne bi oon assent
  A priuey councell al of tresoun,

they would claim Him as theirs, because He'd be of man's nature,

  And clayme ihesu for oure rent:
32 For þat he is kinde of man, it is good chesoun.

¶ Write we his name, wheþer we spede,
  Siþen to us he is vnknowen,

and though of alien begetting, yet sown in Adam's ground, [Page 159.] and to be reaped by them, God notwithstanding.

  For þou3 he be come of straunge seed,
36 3it in adams grounde was he sowen.
  ¶ Whanne he is ripe, do we oure dede;
  Loke we þat we him boþe repe & mowen,
  For þou3 god him silf oure rollis rede,
40 Bi ri3t we chalenge ihesu for oure owne."

The Master Devil undertook to tackle Jesus,

"To me, maistir deuel, it lijs;
  To ihesu wole y take hede,
  To norische him in manye delijs,
44 His freel fleische boþe to cloþe & fede;
  ¶ And þou3 þat he be neuere so wijs,
  3it out of þe wey y wole him lede,

make a fool of him, and bring His soul to hell.

  And make of him boþe fool and nyce,
48 And in helle his soule brede."

¶ þus deuelis þer wilis caste
  Wiþ þer argumentis greete,

For 30 years they tried

  & þritti 3eer þei foondid faste

þE DEUELIS PERLAMENT.

52 To tempte ihesu in manye an hete.   *to tempt Jesus,*
¶ " In to a wildirnes with ihesus y paste,   *and went to a wilderness where*
    Of him knowliche for to gete,
    And fourty daies þere he faste
56 Wiþoute sleep, drinke, or meete."   *he fasted 40 days.*

¶ þe maistir deuel wondre þouȝte   *[Page 160.]*
    Of ihesus stalworþe complexioun ;   *The Master Devil wondered at*
    Bi mannys fode lyuede he nouȝte,   *Jesus' constitution, living only*
60 But bi praiers and deuocioun.   *on prayers; but at last tempted*
¶ "But whanne he bigan to hunger, as me þouȝt,   *Him, 'Here are*
    To tempte him þanne y made me boun :   *stones, make them bread.'*
    ' Lo, heere be stoonys hard y-wrouȝte,
64 Make herof breed, y seide, to mannis foisoun.'

¶ ' Forsoþe,' ihesu seide, ' not oonli in breed   *Jesus said, 'Man's*
    is verrili mannis propir lyuyng,   *food is not bread alone, but every*
    But in euery worde of þe godhede   *word of God.'*
68 To body and soule is coumfortynge.'   *The devil took Him to a pinnacle, leapt down,*
¶ Vpon an hiȝ pinnacle þanne y him brouȝte,   *and asked Him to follow,*
    And left him þere, and leep a-downe,
    And seide, ' saue þee harmelees, lyme & heed,
72 And kiþe now maistries while þou art ȝonge.

¶ If þou be god-is sone, lete se ;   *' Angels shall*
    Of þee is writen longe a-goon,   *bear Thee in their hands lest Thou*
    ' Aungils in hondis schullen beere þee   *strike Thy foot against a stone.'*
76 Lest þou spurne þi foot at a stoon.'
¶ Quod ihesu, ' in holi writt þou maist se,   *[Page 161.] Jesus said,*
    Tempte not þi lord god lyuynge aloone ;   *' Tempt not thy God, but serve*
    Wiþ al þi myght and þi pooste   *Him with all thy might.'*
80 þou schalt him serue, and oþir noone.' "

¶ þe deuel siȝ it myght not geyn ;   *Then the Devil*
    Of ihesu his purpos he gan mys ;   *brought Him to*
    He brouȝte him til an hiȝ mounteyn,   *a mountain,*

	84 And bad him do as he wolde wys.
showed Him all the world's riches, and said,	¶ And þere he schewide him upon þat pleyn, Iewels, ritchesse, and worldli blisse ;
'Worship me, and all this is Thine.'	"Worschipe me here, & bicome my swayn, 88 And y schal ȝeue þee al this."
'Begone, Satan, from heaven!	¶ "Go, sathanas! from blis þou flit, From heuene riche, þat rial tour! It is writen oonli in holi writt
Thy Lord God only shalt thou honour.' Alas, said the Devil,	92 'þi lord god þou schalt honour.'" ¶ "Alas," quod þe deuel, "where hast þou þat witt?
I am sore hit, I never stood such an attack.	þi wordis are bittir, þi werkis aren sour, þi conclusioun so soore me knyt, 96 I abood neuere so scharp a schour."
[Page 162.] Again the Devils held their Parliament in the mist. 'Some one is coming to rifle our home. Once his name was John the Baptist, then Jesus, then Christ.	¶ þe deuelis gadriden þer greet frame, And heelden þer perlament in þe myst. "Oon wolde riflee us at hame, 100 And gadere þe flour out of oure gryst ; ¶ Neewe gilours wolde waite us schame, Oon[ys] men clepid him iohne þe baptist, But now he haþ turned, ihesus is his name : 104 þat first hiȝte ihesu, now is clepid cryst,
He has never sinned in lust,	¶ I siȝ him neuere rage ne plawe, But euere in stabilnes he is ay, And streitely kepiþ god-is lawe,
but has resisted temptation.	108 And stijfly wiþ-stoondiþ myn assay ; ¶ To werkis of vice wole he not drawe ;
He said he would throw down the Temple, and raise it on the third day.	A wondir worde y herde him say, þe greet temple he wolde doun þrawe, 112 And reise it aȝen on þe þridde day.
At His birth	¶ Whanne he was born, wondris bifel : Ouer al was pees, boþe eest and west,

ÞE DEUELIS PERLAMENT.

In rome of oile þere sprong a welle,
116 From tristiuer to tybre it ran prest.
¶ In rome þer templis doun felle,
þer mawmetis diden al to-brest,
Aungils to scheperdis glorie gan telle—
120 'In erþe, to al mankinde, boþe pees & rest.'

¶ Þe emperour in rome stood hiȝe,
þre sunnis in oon he siȝ schyninge clere,
In þe myddis of hem a maiden he siȝe
124 A man childe in her armes beere.
¶ Þe emperour & eek sibile spoken prophesie,
And þei acordiden boþe in feere,
And seiden 'god-is sone mankinde schulde bie;
128 It is þe tokene, þe tyme neiȝeþ neere.'

¶ Also þre kingis come fro fer,
To worschipe ihesu al þei souȝte;
þat reisid eroudis herte þere
132 þem to slee, for þei so wrouȝte.
¶ Bi þe liȝtnynge of a sterre,
To ihesu alle þre presentis þei brouȝte;
Homeward an aungil tauȝte hem nerre
136 A-noþer wey þan þei had þouȝte.

¶ Þanne y councellid eroud with-inne a while
To distroie þe former prophesie,
þat alle men children in towne & pile
140 to slee þem, þat ihesus myght with hem die.
¶ He ascapide in to egipt; in þat while
þer mawmetis fil doun from an hiȝe;
he knew my þouȝte, & siȝ my gilee,
144 y myghte not hide me from his yȝe.

¶ To tempte ihesu it wole not availe;
Of þe worldis good haþ he no neede;

a well of oil sprang up in Rome; temples fell; idols broke. [Page 163.]

Angels announced Peace on earth to all mankind.

The Emperor saw three Suns in one; in their midst a Maid with a child.

He and the Sibyl prophesied, 'God's Son shall redeem mankind; the time draws nigh.'

Three Kings came from far to worship Jesus,

led by the light of a Star, bringing presents

[Page 164.] The Devil advised Herod

to slay all the male children,

but Jesus escaped into Egypt,

detecting the Devil's guile.

'It is no good to tempt Him;

þE DEUELIS PERLAMENT.

the more I work the worse I speed

I leese on him so myche trauaile,
148 þe more y so worche, þe worse y spede;
¶ With þe scharper a-sautis y him assaile,
þe lasse of me he stoondiþ in drede,

and the less He heeds me.

þe bolder in bikir y bidde him bataile,
152 þe lasse of me he takiþ hede.

If I tempt Him

¶ For if y tempte him in wraþþe or pride,
Wiþ pacience and mekenes he sconfitiþ me;

to lechery, He escapes by chastity.

If y tempte him to letcherie, y muste me hide,
156 He voidiþ me of wiþ chastitee.

[Page 165.] He abides in charity, and will not be covetous.

¶ In glotenie & enuye wole he not abide,
But is euere in mesure and in charitee;
In coueitise & auarise wole he not ride,
160 but is euere in largenes and in pouerte."

I can't make him stumble. He never went to school, and yet I saw Him arguing against all the Doctors.

¶ Þe deuel seide, "neiþer in hoot ne coolde
I may not make him stumble ne falle;
I nyste him neuere goo to scolee,
164 And ȝit oonis y siȝ him spute in þe scoole halle:
¶ He satte him silf on þe hiȝest stoole,
And argued aȝens þe maistris alle;
Summe callid him wijs, summe callid him foole,

He calls Himself God's Son.

168 But 'goddis sone' he him silf dooþ calle.

He makes the crooked straight,

¶ Hise werkis passen mannis kinde,
For crokid & creplis he makiþ riȝt;
For deef, & dombe, & boren blynde,

gives sight to the blind, sense to madmen,

172 he ȝeueþ hem speche, heeryng, & sight.
¶ Woode men, he ȝeueþ hem þer mynde,
And makiþ mesels hool and liȝt;

and drives out devils.

A legioun of feendis in a man he dide finde,
176 Alle he drofe out þoruȝ his myght.

[Page 166.] He turns water into wine;

¶ Wiyn of watir he makiþ blyue,
And dooþ manye a wondir dede,

þE DEUELIS PERLAMENT.

    Wiþ two fyschis, and loues fyue,
180 fyue þousand men y saw3 him fede.   *feeds 5000 men with two fishes and five loaves,*
  ¶ Twelue leepis of releef þerof dide þriue
    To men, women, & children, þat hadden nede;   *leaving 12 baskets of fragments,*
    Deed men he reisid from deeþ to lyue,
184 And 3it weriþ he neuere but oo wede.   *and raises the dead to life.*

  ¶ He handliþ neiþer money ne knyf,   *He desires no sin with woman,*
    Neiþer in synne desiriþ he ony woman to kis;
    But oonis he saued a weddid wijf,   *and yet once saved an adulteress.*
188 In spousebriche þat hadde doon mys.
  ¶ He is so wondirful in lijf,   *He is such a wonder I cannot make out what He is. He is out of my books.*
    I can not knowe weel what he is;
    I wolde we hadde eendid oure striif;
192 He is oute of oure bookis, & we out of his.

A fitte. **S**iþen y him first tempte bigan,   *I have never seen him change colour, though once He reproved me.*
    I si3 him neuere chaunge hewe;
    Oonys he bad me "go, foule sathan!"
196 Euere-more þat repreef y rewe.
  ¶ In werkis he is good, in persoone a man;   *[Page 167.] In person He is a man; but where does His knowledge come from?*
    Lijk to him y neuere noon knewe.
    Where lerned he al þe witt þat he can?
200 For euery day he dooþ wondris neewe.

  ¶ I folewide him oonys to a place,   *Once I saw Him with Peter, James, John, Elias, and Moses.*
    To a mounteyne upon an hi3te;
    Petir, iames, & iohn̄, þere was,
204 Ely & moyses stood þere up ri3t.
  ¶ I wolde haue seen ihesu-is face,   *His face shone so bright*
    But y my3t not, it schoon so bri3t;
    In þe sooþfast sunne closid it was,   *that it blinded me.*
208 þe bri3t beemys blent my si3t.

  ¶ To lette þe prophesie soone y went,   *I gave the Jews the choice of killing Jesus.*
    þe iewis to slee ihesu y 3af hem chois;

48   þE DEUELIS PERLAMENT.

If he dies on the cross we are ruined; so I was sorry to hear their 'Crucify Him,' and set Pilate's wife to stop it.

    If he die on þe roode, we schul be schent:
212 I wolde not þat þei hadde ȝeue þat vois.
  ¶ Me was woo for þat iugement,
    Of "crucifuge" to heere þe noise;
    Pilatis wijf y bad bisily ȝeue tent
216 þat ihesu were not doon on þe crois.

[Page 168.] But the Jews bore false witness, and nailed Him on the Cross till He died.

  ¶ Ȝit þe iewis, for hise dedis goode,
    Fals witnes vpon him þei berid,
    And nailed him upon þe roode,
220 And peyned him þere til þat he deied.
  ¶ Vndir his lift side y my silf stood,

I looked sharp after His soul, but couldn't see where it went.

    And aftir his soule ful naruȝ a-spied;
    I wist neuere whidir it ȝode;
224 Whanne he it up ȝaf, so manly he cried;

The sun and moon lost their light, the earth trembled,

  ¶ Þe sunne & moone losten þer light,
    Þe elementis fouȝten as leit of þundir,
    Þe erþe qwoke, and mounteynes an hight,
228 Valeis, & stoonys, bursten a-sundir;

dead men arose.

  ¶ Dede men risen þoruȝ his myȝt
    To bere witnes of þat wondir;

I lost my senses,

    My mynde failid, y loste my siȝte,
232 I nyste how soone y came þer vndir.

and don't know where His soul is gone to.

  ¶ Ihesu is soule is wente, y woot not where,
    So priuely it dide from me passe;
    Whanne his herte was þirllid with a spere,
236 þanne wyste y weel who he was.

[Page 169.] But we must get ready all our tackle, for He'll attack us. Prepare for defence.

  ¶ Ordeyne we us wiþ al oure gere,
    For hidir he þinkiþ to make a race;
    Arise we alle þat ben bounden heere,
240 And foond we to defende oure place,

If He comes we must all try

  ¶ For if þat he wole hidir come,
    We schulen foonde euery-choon,

Alle to-gidere, boþe hool & some,
244 To teer him from þe top to þe toon."
¶ Þanne seide lucifer anoone,
"It is but waast to speken so;
þe spirit of him is now hidir come
248 For to worchen us alle woo."

¶ Þere as þe goode soulis diden in dwelle,
Þei cheyned þe ȝatis, and barred hem faste;
"A! now," ihesu seide, "ȝe princis felle,
252 Openeþ þe ȝatis þat euere schal laste,
¶ And letiþ in ȝoure king of blis to helle."
Þe deuelis axid him þanne in haste,
"Who is þe king of blis þou doost of telle?
256 Wenest þou to make us alle a-gaste?"

¶ "Strong god and king of myght,
I am lord and king of blis,
Ouer-comer of deeþ, myghti in fight!
260 Euerlastynge ȝatis, openeþ wight!
¶ Boþe pees, mercy, trouþe, & right,
I brouȝt them at oon, & made þem to kis;
Euerlastynge ȝatis, openeþ on hight,
264 And lete in ȝoure king to take out his!

¶ For y, þe soule of ihesu crist, am come hider,
Witnes þerof, my body in erþe lieþ deed,
And þe holi goost with þe soule togider
268 Þat neuere schal parte from þe godhede.
¶ In heuen blis ȝe stooden full slidir;
Þoruȝ pride ȝe offendid my fadris bede;
Mannis soule for meeknes schal come þider,
272 Þere as ȝe feendis forfetid þat stide."

¶ Þanne seide lucifer, "god dide forbede
To adam in paradiis but oon tree,

	And peyne of deeþ to haue for þat dede,
Adam to Hell for ever.	276 And aftir in helle euere for to be :
[Page 171.] Thou art of Adam's seed, and we claim Thee. There is no return from Hell.'	¶ And þou art come of adam seed, þerfore bi right we chalenge þee, For in holi writt þou made rede, 280 'In helle is no remedie.'"
'True,' said Christ; 'but the closed Hell is for you; this Hell is free.	¶ Ihesu seide, "lucifer, sooþ þou tellist me ; But þou woost not þi silf how þere is a boonde helle, but þis is free. 284 þe boond helle was ordeyned for ȝou ;
Man is redeemed.	¶ For þat þat man forfetid þoruȝ a tree, þoruȝ a tree aȝen bouȝt is he now.
Thou art condemned.	þou madist him synne, þe peyne longiþ to þee, 288 For þou waitist neuere good to mannis prowȝ.
I sprang not from sinful seed, but	¶ Lucifer, þou me vndir-nome, And seidist y was of þe seed of adams kyn ; forsoþe y out of þe godhede come,
took flesh in a maiden sinlessly.	292 And took fleisch & blood a maiden with-inne. ¶ for as of þe seed of erþe þer springiþ blome, So mette we, & partid wiþoute synne : þin argument is fals, so is þi doome ; 296 Bi what right woldist þou me wynne ?
[Page 172.] When thou temptedst Adam,	¶ Who was cheef of þi councell In heuen whanne þou forfetidist þe blis ? In paradiis adam þou dedist assaile, 300 And temptidist him to forfete his ;
I fought for him,	¶ And y in his quarel took bataile Aȝen my fadir to amende his mys,
and now will defeat thee.'	Wherfor of þi purpos þou schalt faile, 304 forthi þi quarel nouȝt it is."
Lucifer said,	¶ þanne lucifer answeride ageyn, "Whi spekist þou so to me heere ?

ÞE DEUELIS PERLAMENT.

  It is but wantowne wordis in veyn ;
308 I trowe þou comest hidir us to fere.   'Thou comest here to frighten us.
 ¶ Sumtyme whanne y was in heuen an hiȝ,
  Þat þat y þere loste for my pride, certeyn,
  Heere-aftir y hope ful sikirly   I hope to get to heaven again.'
312 For to come to þat blis ageyn."

 ¶ Crist ihesu spak to sathan tho,
  And seide to him in þis manere,   Christ answered,
  " It is but waast to speken so,   'That is idle talk.
316 Or ony suche wordis to seie now here.
 ¶ Þat tyme while þou in heuen were,   [Page 173.]
  Ful myche ioie haddist þou tho ;   While you were in heaven you had
  For alle þi felawis, glad were þei þere,   much joy, but it
320 But riȝt soone it was ouer-goo."   soon ceased.'

 ¶ Lucifer spak to him ageyn,
  And seide to him with wordis sere,   Lucifer said, 'I have dwelt here
  " In þis place y haue dwellid in woo & peine   in torment above 4000 years ; help
324 Moore þan þis .iiij. þousand ȝeere :
 ¶ Helpe me to þat blis ageyn   me to bliss again,
  Þe which y loste for my pride þere,
  for þere it is myrie in certeyn   to merry time with angels.'
328 To wonye wiþ rial aungils clere."

 ¶ " I seie þee, lucifer, y schal þee telle,   Christ answered,
  Or euere ony þing was wrought—   'Before the heavens were
  Heuene or erþe, eir or helle,—   I made thee of nothing,
332 Forsoþe þoo y made þee of nought.
 ¶ In heuen whanne þou stoodist in wele,
  I made þee aboue aungils alle,   and set thee above the angels.
  But þerof rauȝt þou neuere a deel,
336 Suche pride in þin herte gan falle.

 ¶ In heuen whanne þou were at þi wille,   [Page 174.]
  Þou myȝtist haue be in pees & reste ;   In heaven

þE DEUELIS PERLAMENT.

I gave thee my seat when I went away, and when I came back thou

I took þee my seete ful stille,
340 It to ȝeme þou were ful prest;
¶ And while y wente where me list,
And come aȝen a-noon in hiȝe,

said'st thou wast the worthier,

þou seidist þat þou were worþiest,
344 And to sitte þere as weel as y;

and thou never repentedst.

¶ And þou repentidist þee neuermore,
But euere aggregidist þi trespas.

Adam did; he asked mercy. God sent me here for that, and let me die.

Adam wepte & siȝede soore,
348 And askid mercy & oile of grace;
¶ My fadir sende me hidir þerfore,
Vpon a tree leete deeþ me chase,
A spere þoruȝ myn herte gan boore,
352 & leete out þe derworþiest oile þat euere was.

In His name, open your gates.'

¶ In my fadris name of heuene
Opene þe ȝatis aȝens me!"

Like lightning the gates burst.

As liȝt of leite, and þundir leome,
356 þe ȝatis to-burste, and gan to flee;

Christ took out Adam and all His chosen ones; and all sang thanks, namely,

¶ God took out adam and eue ful euene,
And alle hise chosen companye.
þe prophetis seiden with mylde steuene,
360 "A song of wondris now synge we."

Adam,

¶ "A, ha!" seide **Adam**, "my god y se;
He þat made me wiþ his hond!"

Noah,

"I se," seide **noe**, "where comeþ hee
364 þat sauede me boþe on watir & londe!"

Abraham,

¶ Quod **abraham**, "y se my god so free
þat sauede my sone fro bittir bande!"

Moses,

þo seide **moyses**, "þese tablis he bitook me
368 His lawe to preche and vndirstande!"

David,

¶ Quod **Dauid**, "we spoken of oon so grym
þat schulde breke þe brasen ȝatis."

þE DEUELIS PERLAMENT.

  Quod **Zacharie,** " & his folk out nym,   Zachariah,
372 And leue þere stille þo þat he hatis."
  ¶ Quod **symeon,** "he liȝtneþ his folk in dym,   Symeon,
  Lo where derknes schendiþ her statis.
  þo seide **iohne,** " þis lomb, y spak of him,   and John the Baptist.
376 þat al þe worldis synne a-batys."

  ¶ Oure lord them took bi þe hond,   [Page 176.]
  And brouȝt þem to þe place of blis,   Christ led them to bliss, saying he had bought it for all who will
  And seide to them, y vndir-stonde,
380 " þis bargeyn y haue bouȝt her, þis :
  ¶ For riche & pore, free and bonde
  þat wole axe grace and ameende þer mys,   ask grace, and amend their sins.
  Schulen be with ȝou heere pleyande
384 In my kingdom, heuene blis."

  ¶ Thus ihesus crist harewide helle,   Thus Christ harrowed Hell.
  And ledde hise louers to paradijs :   But the other hells he wouldn't touch, where fiends and damned souls ever dwell,
  Of þe oþere hellis wolde he not melle,
388 Where feendis blake bounden lijs,
  ¶ And where dampned soulis euere schulen dwelle
  þat wolen not do weel, but euere be nyce,
  Turmentid with horible deuelis of helle   tormented by horrible devils.
392 þat sumtyme were aungils of prijs.

  ¶ Helle repreued þo þe deuel sathan,   Then Hell reproached Satan with cowardice.
  And horribli gan him dispice,
  " To me þou art a schrewide captayn,
396 A combrid wretche in cowardise."
  ¶ þo seide lucifer, " siþen þe world bigan   [Page 177.]
  I haue brouȝt hidir manye a greet pric   But Lucifer justified himself; he had brought all kinds of men there,
  Hidir into helle of al kinde of man,
400 Boþe þe false, foolis, and þe wise,

  ¶ Helle, so worschipide neuere þou were   and Christ too; but Hell wouldn't
  If þou cowdist haue kept þee soo ;

þE DEUELIS PERLAMENT.

keep them.

   I brouȝte þee boþe god & man in fere ;
404 Whi were þou so nyce to leete him go ?"

Hell said he couldn't help it. Christ took them.

 ¶ Quod helle, " not wiþ þi poowere
  I myȝte not werne him oon of tho ;
  He took out alle þat were him dere ;
408 I myȝte not lette him, þouȝ he wolde mo."

Beelzebub barred up the gates, but Christ broke them through with a word.

 ¶ Quod belsabub, " y barrid ful faste
  þe ȝatis with lok, cheyne, bolt, & pyn ;
  And with oo word of his wyndis blaste
412 þei broken vp, and he came ynne.

 ¶ He boond me, and downe me caste ;
  it is to us no bote to stryue with him ;

After the Doom comes endless torment.

  Whanne þe dreedful doome is come & paste,
416 Oure eendelees peyne is þanne to bigynne."

[Page 178.] Jesus rose on the third day,

 ¶ þouȝ þe iewis dide ihesu to die,
  ȝit on þe þridde day he roos to liif aȝen ;
  It was to him moore victorie
420 þan powȝ he hadde alle þe iewis sleyn.

and was seen by many ;

 ¶ Summe were glad whanne þei him siȝe,
  Summe were sory, summe were fayne,

once in a company of 500.

  And sumtyme in oon companye
424 Amonge .v. hundrid he was seyn.

To Mary Magdalene He said

 ¶ Of oynement ful manye a drope,
  Marie mawdeleyne to ihesu sche brouȝte ;
  Ihesu wente fro a litil a-slope,

'Touch me not,' but to His disciples, 'Handle my wounds; I have flesh and blood, which ghosts have not.'

428 And seide, " mawdeleyn, towche me nouȝt."
 ¶ Alle hise disciplis weren in wanhope ;
  For to coumforte them ihesu þouȝte,
  And bad hem hise woundis handle & grope,
432 " I haue fleisch & blood ! so spiritus haue nouȝt."

To Thomas

 ¶ Thomas was of right hard bileeue
  Til he hadde spoke wiþ ihesu tho :

þE DEUELIS PERLAMENT.

Ihesu spak wiþ wordis breue,
436 " Come hidir, thomas, & speke me to ;
¶ For here þou maist now þe sooþe preue,
How þat y on þe roode was y-doo ;
And he þat wille not on it bileeue,
440 Schal be dampned to peine for euermo."

Jesus said, 'Come and see the proof that I was crucified. [Page 170.] He who will not believe it shall be damned.'

¶ þanne seide ihesu wiþ myelde speche
To hise disciplis, " y wole ȝe goo
To alle creaturis aboute, to preche
444 Myn uprisynge, to freende & foo ;
¶ And þo þat bileeuen þat ȝe teeche,
Bodies and soulis saued ben thoo ;
And þo þat bileeuen not, y seie to eche,
448 þo schulen for euere to peine goo.

To His disciples He said, 'Go and preach my uprising to all people.

They who believe it shall be saved; they who do not shall go to hell.

¶ From ȝou, feendis schulen flee for my name ;
Eddris & venym schal from ȝou steele ;
þouȝ ȝe drinke poisoun, it schal not ȝou tame,
452 Neiþer harme ȝou, ne noo greef feele.
¶ I schal newe tungis in ȝou frame
Alle maner of langagis forþ to deele ;
And þo þat ȝe touche, sike or lame,
456 Body and soule y wole hem heele."

Devils shall flee from you, poison shall not hurt you.

You shall speak all languages, and heal all sick you touch.'

¶ Oure lord, aftir his resurreccioun, here
In erþe he was forsoþe dwellynge
Til hooly þursday comen were,
460 þat he stiȝ to heuene, where he is king.
¶ At þe dreedful doom, wiþ-out lesing,
Boþe quycke and deede þere schal he deme.
God ȝeue us grace in oure lyuynge
464 To serue oure god, & marie to qweeme.

[Page 180.] Christ remained on earth till Holy Thursday, and then ascended into heaven. He shall judge the living and dead.

¶ Of alle þe children þat euere were borun,
Saue oonli crist him silf a-loone,

Next to Christ

the holiest child was John the Baptist, who baptized Christ		Was no on so holi here biforn
	468	As was þis holi child seynt iohun
		¶ Þat baptisid oure lord in flom iordon
		Wiþ ful deuout & good deuocioun,
		And after for ihesus loue to deeþ gan goon,
and died for Him.	472	And suffride ful mykil passioun.

¶ Now schal y telle with ful good cheere
Of þat holi assumpcioun
Of his blessid modir dere,

Christ's blessed Mother was

476 How sche was taken up with greet deuocioun
¶ Vnto hir blessid sone, as his wil were,
Þat þerto sente hise aungils a-down,
& vp þei baren þat maiden cleere;

taken up to her Son [Page 181.]
by angels, and crowned

480 Queene of heuen þere þei dide hir crowne.

Queen of Heaven,

¶ Þenne alle aungils þat were in heuene
Were at þe crownyng of þat maide free,
And songen alle with mylde steuene

while all the angels sang

484 "Gloria tibi domine."

Glory to God.

¶ Þat is a song of ioie and blisse!
God ȝoue us grace þat siȝt to se,
Of his mercy þat we nouȝt mysse,

May we all see that sight!

488 Qui natus es de virgine.

¶ Þis song þat y haue sunge ȝou heere,
Is clepid 'þe deuelis perlament;'
Þerof is red in tyme of ȝeere

This song is called ' The Devil's Perlament,' and is read on the first Sunday in Lent. He who

492 On þe first sunday of clene lent.
¶ Who-so wole haue heuen to his hire,
Kepe he him from þe deuelis combirment;
In heuene his soule may þere be sure

would go to heaven must keep clear of the devil.

496 Wiþ aungils to pleie verament.

[Page 182.] There is no trifling in this tale.

¶ Þis lessoun was made but late;
Þere ben no triflis in þis tale;

þe deuelis boost þus gan he bate,
500 Oure curteis crist, oure king riale.
¶ He helpe us in alle at heuene ȝate,
Wiþ seintis to sitte þere in sale !
Crist ! kepe us out of harme and hate,
504 For þin hooli spirit so special !

Explicit parlamentum of feendis.

This is how Christ humbled the Devil.

May He help us into heaven, and keep us out of harm.

[The *Diatorie* printed in *The Babees Boke*, &c., follows here.]

The Mirror of the Periods of Man's Life,

OR

BIDS OF THE VIRTUES AND VICES FOR THE SOUL OF MAN.

[Lambeth MS. 853, ab. 1430 A.D., pages 120-150, written without breaks, till near the bottom of p. 131, as marked by the insetting of the even lines here.]

<small>Man's birth is wonderful! Begotten in sin,</small>

HOw mankinde doþ bigynne
   is wondir for to scryue so ;
In game he is bigoten in synne,

<small>endangering his mother's life.</small>

4   þe child is þe modris deedli foo ;
Or þei be fulli partide on tweyne,
   In perelle of deeþ ben boþe two.

<small>Poor he comes; poor he goes.</small>

Pore he come þe world with-ynne,
8   Wiþ sorewe & pouert oute schal he goo.

<small>I dreamt I saw a new-born child [¹ Page 121.]</small>

In wyntir nyʒt or y wakid,
   In my sleep y dreemed so ;
I saw a child modir ¹ nakid,
12   New born þe modir fro.

<small>go into the desert, and be taken in hand by an Angel-friend and an Angel-foe.</small>

Al aloone, as god him makid,
   In wildirnesse he dide goo,
Til two in gouernaunce it takid,
16   An aungel freende, an aungil foo.

<small>The *World* told the Child it gave him food and clothes.</small>

Quod þe world to þe child, " how many foolde
   Hast þou brouʒt richesse ? now late se :
Þou schuldist deie for hunger and coolde
20   But y lente meete & cloþe to þee :

THE MIRROR OF THE PERIODS OF MAN'S LIFE.   59

  I wole þee fynde til þou be oolde;   How would he
   How wolt þou quyte it me?"   pay it for them?
  Quod desteine, " he is bouȝt & soolde."
24 Quod deeþ, " his eende make schal we."

  Quod þe child, "y come poore þe world with- *The Child.*
   inne   I came to seek
                    a wondrous
  To pursue a wondirful eritage :   heritage;
  Nakid out of þe wyket of synne,
28 Of the perellis of streite passage,
  To seke deeþ y dide bigynne,   to seek Death;
  Þat ilke dredful pilgrymage,
  Mi body & soule to parte a tweyne,
                    to divorce my soul
32 To make a deuourse of þat mariage. from my body.

  Liȝtnesse, strenþe, corage & bewte,   Bodily gifts, and
   Þe comaundementis þat god bede; God's Commandments,
  Lust, liking, & iolite,   the Pleasures of
                    this life, its
36 .vij. werkis of mercy [1] and þe crede. [1 Page 122.]
  Veyne glorie, flaterynge, and vanyte, Sorrows, and the
                   Works of Mercy,
  Sowowe, siȝing, loue, & drede,
  To the child her seruice profren he,   offer to lead the
                    child to heaven or
40 For helle peyne or heuene meede.   hell.

  Thanne come oon & stood ful stille,   *Freewill says,*
   And his seruice profride he :
  " Þese folke wolde þi silfe spille
44 To make þee bonde; y wole make þee free. I will make thee
                    free;
  Þei han þee tauȝt boþe good & ille;
  From her councel fast þou flee,   leave all others,
  For my name is freewille;
48 Leue alle hem & folowe me."   and follow me.

  The ȝonge childe in studie stood,
   And in herte wittis souȝte.   *Conscience says,*
  Conscience mengid his mood,
52 " Mi fair childe, what hast þou þouȝt?

know evil from good ;		I am Conscience, knowe yuel & good,
		We two to rekenynge must be brouʒt :
Freewill will make thee mad ;		Biwaare ! free wille wole make þee woode ;
	56	Free wille without̄en witte is nouʒt.
know me, Conscience ;		**F**or my name is Conscience ;
		To knowe me þou must bigynne ;
		Discreciou̅n is my science,
[1 Page 123.] cultivate Prudence ;	60	Vicis & Ve̅rtues [1] to voide a twynne.
		A-queynte þe weel with Prudence,
		He lediþ alle ve̅rtues out & inne ;
beware of Recklessness.		Bi waar of richelees, for he wole make diffence,
	64	For he is leder of al synne.
At seven years old the Child		¶ Whanne þe child was .vij. ʒeer olde,
		Passyng sowkyng of milke drewis,
is urged by the Good Angel to		þe good aungil þe childe dide weelde ;
	68	Al vertu to him þan soone he schewis :
honour his parents ;		"To fadir & modir honour þou ʒeelde ;
		Loue god, & drede, and be of good þewis."
by the wicked Angel to despise them ;		þe wickid aungil bad him be boold
	72	To calle boþe fadir & modir schrewis.
by the Good to		**Þ**e good aungil badde him " be mylde
		From al woo, it wole þee werre :
		þat man may hiʒe housis bilde
bridle his tongue ;	76	þat his tunge can weel for-beerre."
by the Wicked to give it license.		Quod þe wickid aungil, "while þou art a child,
		With þi tunge on folk þou bleere ;
		Course of kynde is for ʒouþe to be wilde,
	80	To beete alle children, and do hem deerre."
[1 Page 124.] Childhood lasts from seven		**T**hus at [1] vij. ʒeer age childhood bigynnes,
		And folowith folies many foold ;
		Aftirward his childhode blynnes ;
to *fourteen*.	84	Whanne he is fourtene ʒeer olde,

THE MIRROR OF THE PERIODS OF MAN'S LIFE. 61

    þanne knowliche of manhode he wynnes,
        þe .vij. vertues wiþ him wonne wolde ;
    þanne comeþ þe .vij. deedli synnes
88   With þe wickid aungil housholde to holde.

Then the Seven Virtues and the Seven Mortal Sins strive for the boy's soul.

Quod resoun, " in age of .xx. ȝeer,
        Goo to oxenford, or lerne lawe."
    Quod lust, " harpe & giterne þere may y leere,
92   And pickid staffe & buckelere, þere-wiþ to plawe,
    At tauerne to make wommen myrie cheere,
    And wilde felaẅis to-gidere drawe,
    And be to bemond A good squyer
96   Al nyȝt til þe day do dawe.

About twenty years old, Reason advises man study ; Lust advises music, staff-play, women, and wild companions.

Quod conscience, " þat axiþ coost ;
        þe moore þou spendist, þe lesso þou hast ;
    þi tyme, þi leernynge boþe ben loost,
100   þi freendis good þou spendist in waast."
    Quod lust to conscience, " ȝouþe so muste ;
        ȝouþe can not kepe him chast."
    " Good conscience, goo preche to þe post,
104   þi councel saueriþ not my tast.

Conscience says these will waste time and learning.

Lust poohpoohs that; and the [Page 125.] young Man scorns it ;

Þouȝ Conscience bidde me be stille,
        I wole holde forþe þat y bigan ;
    Al my lust y wole ful-fille,
108   I wole spare no womman ;
    Conscience wolde binde me to skille,
        And make me his bondman.
    Fareweel Conscience ! weelcome frewille !
112   I wole lerne no more good þan y can."

his lust will spare no woman ;

he will not be a servant to conscience, but to Freewill, and learn no good.

Now vicis & vertues wole not slake,
        Now man is .xx. wyntir in age :
    Quod pride, " no man þou forsake,
116   I wole þee sette in þe hiȝest stage."

After twenty years old, come the advice of Pride,

Gluttony,		Quod glotenye, " nyȝt & day þou wake ;
		Ete late & eerli in outrage."
Lechery,		Quod leccherie, " þi seed richelees þou schake,
	120	And make no force of no mariage."
Wrath,		**Q**uod wraþþe, " loke þou bere þee bolde ;
		What man þee teene, His heed þou breest."
Envy,		Quod enuie, " þi foote þou holde,
[¹ Page 126.]	124	And pursue ¹ for to passe þe beest."
Sloth,		Quod slouþe, " in ȝouþe, or þou be oolde,
		Leerne for to take þi reest."
Covetousness,		Quod Coueitise, " wynnen y wolde."
Avarice.	128	Quod auarise, " locke me in þi cheest."
Pride says, wear long pockets, and slashed (?) clothes ;		" **A**pparaile þe propirli," quod Pride,
		" Loke þi pockettis passe þe lengist gise ;
		Slatre þi clothis boþe schorte & side
	132	Passinge alle oþere mennis sise ;
reverence no one,		And where þat þou goo ouþer ride,
		Do no reuerence to foole ne wise ;
oppress the poor, despise advice.		Late no poore neiȝbore þryue þee biside ;
	136	Alle oþer mennis councel loke þou dispise."
Meekness says : Pride will bring you to woe. Once he was lovely in highest heaven,		" **B**i waar," quod Meekenes, " how pride dooþ wys ;
		He ȝeueþ but woo & wyssche to wage ;
		Of aungelis bewte þe prijs was his ;
	140	In heuene on þe hiȝest stage,
		He wolde haue peerid with god of blis ;
now he is loathsome in hell, and meek man has his inheritance.		Now is he in helle moost loþeli page.
		Þat feendis forfetid for her mys,
	144	Is now meeke mannis eritage."
Wrath advises: meddle in every quarrel, [Page 127.]		**Q**uod wraþþe, " From þat councel flee,
		Þou art stalworþe, ȝonge, and liȝte,
		Of all quarellis medle þou þee
wrong or right.	148	Boþe of wronge & of riȝte.

	Who dar bete þee, nay lete be,	
	Riche or poore, weike or wiȝte,	
	Loke þou bere þee boolde on me,	I will bully for you.
152	And y for þee wole chide & fliȝte."	
	Þanne up stood Paciens,	*Patience* warns
	"As wraþþe biddiþ, do not soo,	him against
	For wraþþe haþ no Conscience,	
156	He makiþ ech man operis foo;	Wrath,
	þer-with he getiþ his dispence,	
	þat schulde be freende, to make hem foo.	who makes friends foes.
	Praie god, he be þi diffence,	
160	þat þou be not founde in þe noumbre of þoo."	
	Quod enuie þanne, " y wole þee leere	*Envy* counsels man to whisper evil reports of
	To make þi lord to þee tame;	
	Be homeli, & rowne in his eere,	true men under a promise of secresy.
164	And bringe trewe folk in fals fame.	
	Make him þi suget, to þee to swere	
	þat he schal not discure þi name;	
	So make him fals witnesse to bere,	
168	And gete þee richesse wiþ god-is grame."	
	Þanne up roos a souereyn uertu	
	þat is clepid Charite:	*Charity* says,
	"Loke þou not hise maners sue,	Envy is God's enemy.
172	For god-is enemy soþeli is he.	'Do to others as you would they'd do to you.'
	Do þou to euery man þat is due	
	As þou woldist he dide to þee."	[Page 128.]
	Quod Coueitise " and alle folk were trewe,	*Covetousness*
176	Manye a man schulde neuere þee.	advises man to
	Caste þee faste to Coueitise,	
	Make sotil þi wittis, & forge wilis,	scheme and cheat,
	And preue þat trewe men be nyce,	
180	For so þe fals þe trewe bigilis;	

and so grow rich.	Such beⁿ worschipid & holden wise, þei purchasen hem townes, maners, & pilis, And truþe wolde wite where þi lordschip lijs ; 184 Make heggis bi-twene ȝou, and no stilis."

Bounty in Alms-deeds says, Give to the poor,

    Quod largenes in almesse dede,
      "Couaitise counsolliþ þee amys.
    Ȝeue to þe pore, & þou schalt spede
188   þe bettir, þe gospel seiþ þis ;

and at the Judgment

    For at þe doome þere þou schalt drede,
    Crist wole rehorse of þee y-wys
    þe werkis of merci, as clerkis rede :

you'll go to bliss. 192   If þou hast doon hem, þou goost to blis."

Gluttony says, Love your belly,

    "Man, loue þi wombe," quod Gloteny,
      "Leie mete upon meete, & ete faste ;
    But leue not þi crummes drye,

eat and drink; 196   Drinke þou til þe ful flood be paste.

fornicate, and never fast. [Page 129.]

    Leue clennesse, & use harlotrie,
    But neuere a day loke þou ne faste ;
    In þi wombe make þi tresorie,
200   Of þeeuis þanne þou schalt not be agast."

Moderation says, Gluttony makes

    Quod Mesure, "man ! haue me in mynde.
      God made man suget to resoun :

men beasts, and

    Wat turneþ a man to beestis kinde
204   But etynge & drynking out of sesoun ?

drunkenness blinds their souls.

    Drunkelew folk ben goostli blinde ;
    For faute of witt her lijf is gesoun ;
    In ydil ooþis wasten þei her wynde :
208   To repreue suche, god fyndiþ enchesoun."

Sloth says, Never go to church, don't mind good advice,

    Quod Slouþe, "bisynesse y þee forbede ;
      To chirche neiþer goo ne renne ;
    Who techiþ þee good, take noon hede,
212   Aȝens oo worde ȝeue him ten :

THE MIRROR OF THE PERIODS OF MAN'S LIFE. 65

Seie 'alle folk ben not sotil in dede;'
Excuse þee so bi oþer men,   *excuse yourself*
And ȝeue hem myche maugre to mede   *by others'*
216   þat ony good þee wolde kenne."   *example.*

Quod Besinesse, "man! of Slouþe be waare;   *Business warns*
He is assigned to helle for synne;   *man against Sloth.*
In good lyuynge þi wittis ware,
220   To drede god þou muste bigynne;   *Fear God, and*
þi fleischeli lustis þou muste spare,   *deny your lusts.*
For vicis and vertues wole voide atwynne;   [Page 130.]
In besinessis hous is good weelfare,   *Business brings*
224   And Slouþe haþ hunger and cloþis þinne."   *welfare.*

Quod leccherie to man, "loue þanne weel me,   *Lechery says:*
þi lustis with wommen þou fulfille,   *Satisfy your lust with women;*
For if þou in ȝouþe sparist þanne þee,
228   þou maist falle in greet perille.
Ȝouþe ful of corage wole be;   *youth will be gay.*
þou muste haue helpe, or ellis spille;
Spare no womman, y councelle þe,   *Spare no woman.*
232   þouȝ summe cryen neuere so schille."

Quod Chastite to man, "loo,   *Chastity warns*
Herken how leccherie dooþ speke!   *man that Lust*
Whanne þou þi foule luste hast doo,   *when gratified will threaten him with*
236   Bi waare him þanne! he wole þee prete,
And seie 'for þou hast so doo
þou must suffre peynes greete;'   *torments, and*
And but if god help þee þo,   *he'll fall into despair.*
240   Soone in wanhope he wole þee lete.

Quod þe good aungil, "ȝit þee avise;   *The Good Angel*
Lerne witte while þou art heere;   *tells man to consider,*
He is a foole þat may be wise,   *and not be a fool,*
244   In heuene comeþ no foolis to ȝeere,   [Page 131.]

as God refuses reckless fools.		God doiþ richelees foolis refuse þat kunnen no good, ne noon wole lere ; If wordis excuse, werkis accuse,
	248	þat makiþ hem worse þan þei were."
At *thirty* years old, man boasts of his powers.		"IN þritti ȝeer now y abide ; In discrecioun I haue in-siȝt, Loueli to goo, and to ride,
	252	Ful of manhode & of myȝt."
Conscience reproves him for his vices,		Quod Conscience, "vertues þou puttist aside, And norischist vicis day & nyȝt." Quod man in scorn, "lo, Conscience doþ chide!
	256	For losse of catel he dar not fiȝt."
and shows him the cost of Pride,		"Man, kepe þi richesse," quod Conscience, "To maynteine pride, it costiþ greete ;
(as against Meekness),		It costiþ nouȝt, meekenesse ne pacience,
	260	But it axiþ greet coost to chide & to beete.
of Lechery,		Leccherie axiþ greet dispense,
Gluttony,		It distroieþ mannis kindeli heete ; And glotenie coostiþ wiþouten diffence
	264	Boþe in diuerse drinkis and meete.
		IT costiþ greet to use a synne
Envy,		þat is clepid foule Enuye,
[Page 132.]		For it fretiþ man with-inne ;
	268	Bodi & soule it doþ distroie.
Sloth,		Slouþis þrifte, it is ful þinne, It costiþ myche in slouþe to lie ;
Covetousness, and Avarice.		And Coueitise al þe world wolde wynne,
	272	And Auarise aftir more doith crie."
Man justifies himself. Youth must do folly, or Age would have no wisdom.		Quod man to Conscience, "ȝouþe axiþ delice ; For ȝouþe þe course of kinde wole holde ; But ȝouþe were a foole and nyce,
	276	How schulde wijsdom be founde in oolde.

þe corage of ȝouþe, and oolde wise,
Makiþ ȝonge men to be boolde;
In witt of oolde, worschipe lijs;
280   In þe witte of wise, kingdom is holde.

Þou wastist þi wynde & spillist þi speche,   '*I hate to hear
þi wordis me is looþ to heere;   you, Conscience,
And y dide as þou doist me teche,   trying to stop my
                                                 merry-making.*
284   I schulde neuere make myrie chere.
Wenest þou with þin hond heuene to reche?
   þin arme wole not be so longe to ȝeere;
Now, good Conscience, & þou wolt preche,   *If you will preach,
                                                 steal a cowl and*
288   Goo stele an abite, & bicome a frere."   *be a friar.*

Quod man, y pleie, y wrastile, y sprynge,   [Page 133.]
þese ioies wolen neuere wende me fro;   *I play and wrestle,*
Now alle gamys hom y brynge;
292   What such as y am, þer ben no moo:
I leepe, y daunce, y skippe, y synge,   *dance and sing,
                                                 and never cry*
I am so myrie y can not seie hoo."   *Halt!'*
Quod Conscience, "þou schalt weepe & wringe   *Conscience.
                                                 "You'll weep*
296   Whanne þei take her leeue to goo."   *when that's
                                                 over."*

"**M**yn iȝen ben cleere & briȝt as glas,   *Man.
                                                 'My eyes are*
Mi lire as lillye and roose of hewe,   *bright, and I'm*
Of schappe & strengþe alle folke y passe,
300   And euere my uertu wexiþ newe."   *stronger than any
                                                 other man.'*
Quod Conscience, "y loue þee weel þe lasse,   *Conscience.
                                                 "You do no good*
þou usist no werkis of good vertu."   *works."*
"Goo, Conscience, þou lewide asse,   *Man.
                                                 'Conscience,*
304   I kepe not þi maneris to sue."   *you're an ignorant
                                                 ass.'*

Quod man, "Myne age is fourti ȝeere."   *At forty years
                                                 old, man is ad-*
Quod þe world, "y offre to þee my weele."   *vised by the
                                                 World,*
Quod strengþe, "late no man be þi peere."   *Strength,*
308   Quod corage, "late no man with þee deele." *Courage,*

5 *

[Page 134.] Lust, Health,		Quod luste and liking, "make good cheere."
		"I am al hool wiþ þee," quod heele.
Conscience,		Quod Conscience, "wistist þou what þese were?
	312	At nede wole faile þi fleische so freele."

Quod Conscience to man in ȝouþe,
"Traueile in troupe in tyme is beste."

and Truth. Gat riches in youth that shall do for age.
316 Quod troupe, "gete þee richesse nouþe
Wherwiþ in oolde to haue þi reste;
þouȝ age can as he cowthe,
Myȝt & corage he haþ looste,
He kepiþ his soule þat kepiþ his mouþe,
320 For þe soule to þe fleisch is but a goost."

At *fifty* years old,
"**N**Ow am I fifti ȝeere y-wis,
Myn heer bigynneþ to change his hewe."

Conscience tells man to do good works.
Quod Conscience, "flee from alle vice,
324 And use werkis of good vertu,
Late not þi werkis preue þee nyce,
Loke þat þou euere be founden trewe."

He prefers covetousness.
"Fare weel Conscience, weelcome Coueitise!
328 To be richee now y wole pursue."

[Page 135.] Conscience dissuades him; Overhope makes him sin;
Quod Conscience, "þat is idil bisynesse,
Nedelees richesse to gadre soo;
Ouerhope is þe cause y-wisse,
332 He weneþ ameende al er he goo."

Despair helps too.
Wanhope seiþ, "kepe weel þis,
For þe world wole faile us two."
Quod Conscience, "chaunge not heuen blis
336 For helle peyne, sorowe, and woo."

At *sixty* years old, man laments his evil doings.
"**I**N sixti ȝeere myn age is piȝte,
Myn iȝen daswen, myn heer is hoore;
In my werkis y haue febil in-siȝte,
340 I fynde no vertu in my stoore.

How schal y reckene with god almyȝt?
I am aschamed wondir soore."
Quod Conscience, "certis it were riȝt
344   To be holi now or neuere moore."   *How shall he reckon with God? "Be holy now or never."*

Quod ȝouthe to age, "what doist þou nowþe?
Hange up þin hachet & take þi reste;
þe sunne is past fer bi þe sowthe,
348   And hiȝeth swiþe in to þe weste."
Quod man, "y serued þee in ȝougþe
And al þe tyme myne eruest leste,
Wiþ sorowe of herte & schrifte of mouþe
352   To god ȝit haue y kepte þe beste."   *Youth taunts the old man: he is past and gone. [Page 136.] The old man repents and will serve God.*

"**A**ge, calle aȝen ȝistirday to-morowe;
And alle þi werkis, bigynne hem newe."
Quod man, "þouȝ þou speke in scorne,
356   þou techist me good þat y neuere knewe;
I wole biþinke me on my werkis biforn,
Do almes dede, praie, & rewe,
And goddis mercy schal ynne my corn,
360   And fede me wiþ þat þat y neuere sewe.   *Youth mocks him again. The old man learns from the scorn, will pray and sorrow, and God will in his corn.*

In ȝougþe whanne y was wilde & stronge,
þe fals world fair dide me wowe,
Me þouȝt ech worde a myrie songe,
364   Wiþ pipis, and dauncis, & mirþis ȝ-nowe.
Now seiþ he, he loued me to longe,
For myn heer bigynneþ to blowe;
To þi mercy, lord, me vndirfonge,
368   þe tyde is ebbid, & no more wole flowe."   *'When young, the false world wooed me, but in age has left me. Have mercy on me, Lord.*

"**Þ**e candel of lijf þi soule dide tende:
To liȝte þee hom," resoun dide saye.
"Miche of my candel in waaste y spende,
372   Manye wickid windis haþ wastid it away;   *[Page 137.] My candle of life I let winds of wickedness waste;*

I can scarcely hold its end.		Vnneþe y holde my candelis eende,
		It is past euensonge of my day;
		To reepe myn heruest, whidir mai y winde?
	376	Mi londis of vertues liggen al lay.
		¶ Whanne ȝouþe was maistir, y was page,
I lived in the Devil's service, with late suppers and late rising.		We lyueden myche in þe feendis seruice,
		Wiþ rere souperis and wickid outrage,
	380	Ligge longe in bed, looþe to arise.
Now the wise reprove me, and		Now haue y nouȝt but wisschis to wage,
		And myche repreef amonge þe wijse;
former friends hate me.		þei þat loueden me in ȝouþe, hatiden me in age.
	384	And vnkindeli me diden dispice.
I wonder why the world was made.		Now haue y greet meruaile
		þe world to man whi it was wrouȝte;
		Fele temptaciouns now me assaile,
I have no rest,	388	I haue no reste for chaunge of þouȝte.
[Page 138.]		Whanne y schulde reste y haue greet merueile;
		In bed to sleepe whanne y am brouȝte,
and see nothing but battle and dread.		I se but drede and greet bataile
	392	Al mannys lijfe, and it be souȝte.
The world has forsaken me;		Thus þe fals world haþ forsaken me;
		For waste of hise goodis he accusiþ me;
my sins accuse me		þe synnes þat y loued, now haten me,
	396	To Conscience þei adwiten me;
fiends threaten me;		Feendis preten faste to take me,
		And steren helle houndis to bite me;
Death shakes his spear at me.		Deeþ seiþ, my breed he haþ baken me;
	400	Now schakeþ he his spere to smite me.
I am like a stag at bay.		Þus y am huntid as an herte to a-bay,
		I not whidir y may me turne,
		Myne enemyes myȝtili me assay,
	404	I waxe feble and vnourne;

To flee to god is my beste way, I will flee to God.
þere schal y in no poynt spurne ;
Lord ! now socour me þat beste may, Lord, help me!
408 In þin herte blood, þat holi bourne."

Quod ȝouþe to age, " y þee forsake, [Page 139.]
Youth taunts Age
with his failing
strength
þi frendis deien, þi strengþe dooþ faile,
þi siȝte and heeryng bigynneþ to slake,
412 þee nediþ helpe and good counsaile ;
God-is seruauntis in areest haþ þee take and Death's ad-
vance on him.
He must make up
his accounts
quickly.
Til deeþ on þee haue doon bataile ;
þi reckenyng bi tyme bisili þou make,
416 Or þe deuel bringe þe countirtaile."

Þouȝ deeþ be eende of worldlis woo, To some Death
here is a friend,
þanne deeþ is euere mannys freende ;
thouȝ soulis in helle be ponischid soo, but not to any in
hell.
420 Deeþ comeþ not þere to make noon eende ;
Deeþ makiþ soulis to heuen to goo, It sends some to
heaven, and there
troubles them not.
But in to heuen deeþ may not wende,
For deeþ is flemyd heuene froo,
424 Deeþ is sugett to god to bende.

"**N**ow y am sixti ȝeere and ten, At *seventy* years
old, the man feels
in the way of
young folk;
Ȝonge folke Y fynde my foo,
Where euere þei pleie, leepe, or renne,
428 þei þinken in her weie Y goo ;
And whanne y mete with olde men, [Page 140.]
his only comfort
is in complaints,
and telling other
old men his
troubles.
I pleyne ' þis world is chaungid soo ; '
Noon oþer bote is but seelde when
432 Ech man telliþ oþir his woo."

Quod ȝouþe to age, " y þee a-peele Youth accuses
him of
And þat bifore oure god y-wis ;
I lente þee strengþe, bewte, & heele,— wasting his
strength
436 þese percellis ben of heuen blis,—

and wealth	Corage, liʒtnesse, freendis, & weele ;
	Alle þese þou hast wastide amys
in folly,	From wijsdom in-to folies feele :
	440 God wole haue rekenyng of al þis.
his sight in vainglory, his mouth in oaths and gluttony,	Þine heerynge and þin iʒe siʒte þat þou hast wastide in veynglory ; þi mouþe to wronge aʒen riʒte,
	444 In fals ooþis and foule gloteny ;
his hands in robbery,	þin hondis to robbe and to fiʒte ; þi strengþe þou wastidist in tyrauntry ;
his beauty in lechery.	þi feet in derknesse oute of liʒte,
	448 þi bewte þou wastidist in lecchery."
[Page 141.] The old man confesses his shortcomings,	Quod man, "y was gouerned Bitwene two þeuis, þei stale on me : Y was stalworþe & white ; Whanne my leepis weren brouʒt to preuis,
	452 I wondre on my silf Y was so liʒte.
regrets his loss	ʒougþe staale from me ; þat soore me greuis ; Age steeleþ on me boþe day and nyʒte ;
of youth and power,	Mi ʒougþe, my vertu, al from me meuis ;
	456 Now wondre y on my silf where is my myʒte.
and complains how youth, with all its glory, has stolen from him, and age, with all its defects, has stolen upon him.	¶ ʒougþe staale from me, Y was stalworþe & liʒte ; And age steeleþ on me Filþis to weelde ; ʒougþe steeliþ from me, Y ʒeede up riʒte ;
	460 Age steeleþ on me, Y bowe and ʒeelde ; ʒougþe haþ stolen from me My leepis liʒte ; Age steeliþ on me, Y wexe on-mylde ; ʒougþe steeleþ my corage To pleie & fiʒte,
	464 Age is so on me stoolen þat y mote to god me ʒilde.
At *eighty* years old	"Now y am euene of ʒeeris fore scoure, So manye wyntir Y am oolde ; þere y was wonte To leepe bifore,
	468 Fer aboute now My wei y hoolde :

THE MIRROR OF THE PERIODS OF MAN'S LIFE. 73

  My backe bowiþ, myn iȝen ben soore,   [Page 142.]
  Myn hoote blood is kelid coolde :   his back is bent,
  Alas ! Conscience ! to litil y toke þi loore,   his hot blood cold.
472 þe talis þat þou hast ofte me toolde."   Ah, Conscience ! I did not listen to you.

  Quod Conscience, "where haddist þou þat speche?   Conscience
  þi liȝte leepis foonde to preue ;   wonders at the man's repentance,
  þe put of þe stoon þou maist not reche,
476 To litil myȝte is in þi sleue.
  In yougþe whanne y dide þee teche,
  Foule þou me þanne dedist repreue ;
  I þanke god of þi good leeche."   but thanks God for it.
480 "Ȝhe, Conscience, now to þi wordis y leeue."

  "**N**Ow foure score ȝeeris is past,   At *ninety* years old man's life is but woe,
  Mi lijf is but traueil & woo,
  Fer in to rereage y am cast,
484 Into ten ȝeer and moo.
  My lymes foulden þat weren fast,
  Wiþ staffe in honde now y goo ;   he walks with a staff,
  My redy speche may not last,
488 So my teeþ ben fallen me fro.   his teeth fall out,

  Ful of fleissche Y was to fele,   [Page 143.]
  Now may I neiþer stonde ne goon ;   his flesh is gone,
  It haþ now lefte me euery dele,
492 Me is lefte But skyn & boon.   he is but skin and bone,
  Now y am vndre Fortunes whele,
  My frendis forsaken me Euerychoon,   forsaken by his friends,
  And alle þe synnes Y loued so weel,
496 Now wote y weel þei been my foon."   and his sins his foes.

  Quod course of kinde, "What helpiþ, y wende,   Course of Nature asks the good of
  þi wissching And þin hadde-y-wist ?   his vain regrets.
  What maist þou On þo wordis spende,
500 It is ful febil In þi fist.

All men expect his death, and none will regret him; he cumbers all.	Now alle men waiten aftir þin eende; þou3 þou deye, þou schalt not be myste; þou combrest boþe foo & frende, 504 þi mylle haþ grounde þi laste griste."
These mortal sins must quit the aged:	Þre deedli synnes maden her moone, " We forsaken man in age."
Pride,	Quod Pride, "y am from him goon, 508 For Pride in age Doiþ disperage."
Lechery, [Page 144.]	Quod leccherie, " He loueþ to lie a-loone; þou3 he wolde do, him wantiþ corage."
Gluttony.	Quod Glotenie, " he is but felle & boone, 512 He loueþ more mesure þan outrage."
Two think him no good, Envy and Wrath.	Quod Envie, " age hath no my3te Ne richesse, lenger me to fynde." Quod wraþþe, " age may not fi3te 516 þou3 he be angri, bi course of kynde."
Two claim him, Sloth and Covetousness.	Quod Slouþe, " age my chaumbre haþ di3te, And calleþ me ease in his mynde." Quod Coueitise, " age haþ me hi3te; 520 Suget to me he dooþ him binde."
Overhope, or vain Confidence that they will ever do well, is the cause of men's waste and sin. Then comes Sickness.	" I knowe," quod ouerhope, " fleissch is freele, Of oolde and 3onge, of man, of childe; In ouerhope þei wasten her weele, 524 And in diuerse werkis ful wylde; þei ouerhope euere to lyue in heele, From age & sijknesse þei weneþ hem schilde,
Then Wanhope or Despair,	þanne comeþ sijknesse, & printiþ his seele." 528 Quod wanhope " þan y make him mylde;
[Page 145.] and bids them hoard. Overhope still lures them on;	I bidde him horde, and richesse saue, For wanhope after mischife doiþ waite, Whanne sijknesse comeþ men to craue," 532 Quod ouerhope, " þan y flatir, & sumtyme flaite,

  'þou schalt lyue, and þi silf it haue.'"
  "Ȝhe," seiþ wanhope, "kepe it straite,   *Despair* mocks them,
  Of good hope no co*u*ncell þou craue
536 Til deeþ þee caste wit*h* a trippe of dissaite."

  Quod wanhope, "a gospel y radde :   and tells them the Gospel; if they
   To telle it þee y wole bigynne,
  'If a ma*n* in sy*n*ne be sadde   will plunge daily into sin, God will
540 Ech day newe, and lieþ þer-inne,   be more pleased than if they never
  Of such a ma*n* god is moore gladde   sinned.
  þan of a childe þat neu*er*e dide synne."
  Q*u*od Conscience, "he wolde make þe madde   *Conscience*
544 To repente þee not, ne neu*er*e blynne."

  Quod Conscience to wanhope, "I-wys   reproves Despair,
   þou liest, y hate þe þ*er*fore ;
  I knowe þe gospel, it seiþ þis,   and repeats the true Gospel, that
548 'If a man haue sy*n*ned longe bifore,   of a repentant
  And axe m*er*cy A*nd* a-mende his mys,
  Repente, and wilne to sy*n*ne no more,   sinner God is gladder than of
  Of þat man god gladder is   [Page 146.] one who never
552 þan of a child sy*n*lees y-bore.'"   sinned.

  Quod wanhope, "a gospel y radde ;   *Despair* urges the Gospel that
   What it meneþ y can expownde,   men suffer as they
  Ech man schal haue peine or meede,
556 In þouȝte or dede as he is founde ;   are found, and as the old man has
  He haþ not ȝit repentid his dede,   notyetrepented,he
  He siȝkeþ for sy*n*nes ben not vnbou*n*de ;
  þouȝ mercy come, he schal not spede,   cannot get mercy.
560 For in daung*er* of wa*n*hope he is bounde."

  Qu*o*d Conscience, "þou dotid hoore !   Conscience says, 'Doted whore,
   God-is m*er*cy þou woldist distroie ;
  þou wenest þi wickidnesse were moore   God's mercy
564 þan god-is goodnesse & his mercie.

THE MIRROR OF THE PERIODS OF MAN'S LIFE.

<small>is enough for a thousand worlds if they ask it.'</small>

For if a man be woundid soore,
 And axe no medicine, him liste te deie ;
 God haþ mercies y-now in stoore
568 For a þousand worldis þat mercie wole crie."

<small>The *Old Man* calls on the Virtues to befriend him in his need.</small>

"MEkenes, Pacience, and Charitee,
 ȝe þat weren my frendis dere,
 Mesure, Bisinesse, and Chastitee,
572 At þis mystire comeþ me neere."
 Quod Conscience, " þou flemed us from þee ;
 þou woldist not oure loore leere."

<small>[Page 147.]</small>

<small>Recklessness offers instead, the crew of Sins that he loved.</small>

Quod richelees, "loo, heere my meynee !
576 þe synnes þat þou louedist & seruedist, lo hem
 here ! "

<small>At a *hundred* years old man carries his bier on his back, all his friends wish him dead.</small>

"Myne age is now an hundrid ȝeere ;
 Litil y drinke, and lesse y ete,
 On my backe I bere my beere,
580 And alle my frendis me forȝete,
 Fayn þei wolde þat y deed were,
 Wiþ sorewful wordis þei doon me þretee,
 And seyn, ' for y am so longe heere,
584 Whanne y come hoome y schal be beete.'

<small>He may stretch out his neck for Death's sword ;</small>

NOw mote y leie forþ my necke,
 For deeþ his swerd out haþ lauȝte ;
 But I deliuere weel þis checke,
588 I leese my game at þis drauȝte.

<small>he is full of sin ;</small>

Ful of synne is my secke ;

<small>he must go to wreck</small>

To þe preest y wole schewe þat frauȝte,

<small>unless God have mercy.</small>

Mi schip is chargid, al gooþ to wrecke
592 But if god of merci be wiþ me sauȝte."

<small>The World reproves him,</small>

This worlde haþ me in awaite,
 And biddiþ me quite þat is past ;

<small>Overhope and Despair tempt him,</small>

My fleissche in ouerhope wolde me faite,
596 And into wanhope it wolde me caste.

	Helle houndis berken and baite,	[Page 148.]
	þe feendis writiþ my synnes faste,	Hell-hounds bark for him, the Fiends and Death watch for him.
	And deeþ me waitiþ with a trippe of dissaite;	
600	These sixe maken me soore agaste."	

Þanne comeþ forþ good hope: But *Good Hope*
    To saue man he wolde fonde;   will save the old man,
"Þou wronge weuere ouerhope!
604   I make him free, þou woldist make him bonde;
I schal conclude þee, þou wanhope,
    Wile good feiþ wole with me stoonde;   if Good Faith will help.
Hooli writte seiþ, 'in god y hoope,
608   His merci is ouer þe werkis of his honde."

Quod good feiþ, "for þe litil while   Good Faith will
    þat now heere [þou] hast serued me,
I wole þee kepe from al perile,   make his peace with God,
612   And make pees bitwene god & þee;
And ouerhope, for al his gile,   and drive out
    From þin herte.y schal do him flee;
And wanhope also y wole exile,   Overhope and
616   For he is not of oure fraternitee."   Despair.

Quod þe worlde, Y wole hise dettis quyte,   Man says he will
    And oute of his daunger me hyȝe;
þouȝ my fleissche berke, he schal not bitee,   give up his fleshly
620   From his lustis y wole him tye;
I wole waissche a-¹Wey þat feendis write   [¹ Page 149.]
    With sorowe of herte and teer of yȝe,   lusts, will sorrow and weep,
But with deeþ y wole not dispuite,
624   But make me cleene, and leerne to deie.   and learn to die.

God! sowe þi merci amonge my seede,   May God sow His mercy in
þanne schal it growe þouȝ y sowe late,   him,
And Repentaunce my corne schal weede,   and Repentance will weed his
628   And make good pees þere was hate.   corn.

	þe comaundeme*n*tis þat god bede,
	þat is þe locke of heue*n* ȝate ;
Then the works of Mercy will let him in at heaven's gate.	Seuene w*er*kis of mercy, and þe crede,
632	þese keies schullen late me in þe*r*ate."
Reader, you have heard of Youth and Age, Virtue and Vice, Good Angel and Bad.	**N**ow haue ȝe herde of ȝouþis delice ;
	And age in kynde, sijke, & woo ;
	Knowi*n*g of ue*r*tu & of vice ;
636	Good aungil, & wickid freende, & foo ;
	And vndirstondi*n*ge to be wijs.
	Now in þis mirro*ur* loke ȝ*o*u soo ;
Look in this Mirror; take your choice, for Heaven or Hell.	In ȝoure free wille þe choice lijs,
640	To heue*n* or helle whiþir ȝe wille goo.
The world, the flesh, and the devil tempt us.	**T**he worlde, þe fleissche, & þe feende,
	In te*m*ptacion*n* doiþ us chase ;
	Bid repentau*n*ce to m*er*ci beende,
644	And waissche us at þe welle of gr*a*ce.
[Page 150.] Let us pray to God , that after death we may see His fair face.	Praie we to god grau*n*te us good eende,
	And in heue*n* to haue a place,
	þat after ou*r*e deeþ we mowen þidir wende,
648	And in p*er*fiȝt loue se his fair face.
Dear friends, who read this, pray for the Writer's soul to Mary, Mother,	**N**ow, leeue freendis, greete and smale,
	þat haue herde þis trete,
	Praie for þe soule þat wroot þis tale
652	A Pater n*os*ter, & an aue
	To marie modir, maiden free,
	As sche bare a childe Cou*m*forte to us,
to pity it if Christ will. Amen.	On þat soule haue pitee
656	If þe wille be of crist ih*es*us. **amen.**

[*Stans Puer*, printed in *Babees Boke*, &c., p. 27, follows here.]

God send us Paciens in oure Oolde Age!

[*Pages* 113—17, *written without breaks.*]

  FRom þe tyme þat we were born
   oure ȝouþe passiþ from day to day,   Our youth passes
  And age encreesiþ moore & moore,   away from day
4 & so doiþ it now, þe sothe to say :   to day,
  At euery hour a poynt is y-loore,
   So fast goþ oure ȝouþe away,
  And ȝouþe wole come aȝen no moore,   and 'will come back
8 But age wole make us boþe blak & gray.   no more,
  þerfore take hede boþe nyȝt & day   Take heed, then,
   How fast ȝoure ȝouþe doþ asswage ;
  And boþe ȝonge & oolde, lete us praie   and pray God for
                   patience in old
12 þat god send us paciens in oure oolde age.   age.

¶ Age wole take from us oure myȝt   Age will take from
  þat in oure ȝouþe to us was lent ;   us
  And also þe cleernesse of oure syght   our clear sight,
                   hearing,
16 And oure heerynge schal be faynt.
  þanne schulen we be heuy þat eer were liȝt,   and lightness.
   Bicause þat ȝouþe is from us went,
  And þanne wole men do us no riȝt,
20 But al contrarie to oure entent,
  And sikenes wole do us greet turment   Sickness will
   Whom deeþ wole sende on his message ;   torment us.
  Forsoþe þe best ameendement
24 is þanne pacience in oure olde age.   [Page 114.]

Our bones will ache,	**O**ure body wole icche, *oure* bonis wole ake,
	oure owne fleisch wole ben *oure* foo ;
our head shake,	Oure heed, *oure* hondis, þo wolen schake,
	28 And oure leggis wole tremble where we go ;
	Oure bonis wole drie as doop a stake,
	And in *oure* bodi we schulen be woo,
our nose turn black,	Oure nose, *oure* chekis, wolen wexe al blake,
	32 & oure glad chere wole fade us fro ;
	And whanne oure teeþ ben goon also,
our tongue lose its fair speech,	Oure tunge schal lese his fair langage :
	Praie we for us silf & oþer moo
	36 . þat god sende us paciens i*n* oure olde age !
Our friends will hate us ;	**O**ure freendis þat schulden loue us best,
	þanne wole þei haue us b*ut* in hate,
	In freendschip is þer noo*n* oþer trust,
	40 & þerof be we waare to late.
we shall say, 'Oh, if I had but known ; ' no kiss will greet us	þan may we synge of had y wist,
	Oure feynt freendis han us forsake,
	And also we schulen go vnkist
	44 boþe at þe dore & at þe gate ;
and no joy gladden us. [¹ Page 115.] God send us patience in our old age !	And for al þe cheer þat we can make,
	þan is ¹ no ioie of *oure* visage :
	Whanne *oure* bewte schal aslake,
	48 god send us paciens in *oure* olde age !
	¶ we schulen be so ang*ri* euermore,
	we wolden ben awreke of euery wrong,
Some will scorn us, others think we live too long ;	þanne summe wolen scorne us þerfore,
	52 & summe wole seie we lyue to long ;
our stomachs will take no food ;	Oure sorowe wole þan sitte us so soore
	Oure stomak wole no mete fonge ;
	& eueri day more & more
we shall sing of sorrow and care.	56 Of sorewe & care schal be *oure* song.
	whanne we were boþe hool & strong
	we were to wie[l]de, & wold out rage,

And þerfore lete us praie among
60   þat god send us paciens in oure olde age.

¶ For þan wole no þing us availe
    but oure bedis and oure crucche,
    for wordli welþe wole fade & faile,
64   And þerfore truste we it not to myche ;
    & þan wole sijknes us assaile
    Til it haþ made us lijk a wrecche,
    & þan may we do no greet traueile
68   But ¹summtyme grone, & sumtyme grucche,
    And sumtyme clawe for scabbe & icche
    Whanne age haþ us at his auauntage :
    Who-so lyueþ long schal be such ;
72   God sende us paciens in oure olde age !

¶ Al þat we haue lyued heere,
    It is but as a dreem y-met,
    For now it is as it neuere were,
76   And so is it þat is to comyng ȝit.
    Ful fast we drawen to oure beere,
    In sorewe & drede we schulen be sett.
    Of oolde men þe ȝonge may lere,
80   And fewe þer ben þat doon þe bett ;
    For þe feend haþ cauȝt hem in his nett,
    And holdiþ hem fast in bondage
    For þei schulden not dispose her witt
84   To haue pacience in her oolde age.

¶ Þanne schulen we se þat worldli blis
    Is but a þing of vanite,
    And it makiþ men to do amys
88   þat ben in weelþe & greet bewte ;
    And þerfor, lord, good riȝt it is
    With oure owne staf chastisid to be :
    Lord ! ȝeue us grace to þinke on þis,
92   As þou bouȝt us alle upon a tree,

Let us pray God to send us Patience in our old age.

Nought but prayers and a crutch will then avail us,

for sickness will assault us,

[¹ Page 116.] and we shall groan and get the itch.

May God send us Patience then !

Our time on earth is but as a dream ;

we draw towards our death.

Let the young learn from the old, for the devil keeps them

from having Patience in their old age.

Then worldly bliss will seem vain.

It is right that we be chastised with our own staff. Christ, let us think on this,
[Page 117.]

> *And* þat we may in charite
> Weel passe ou*er* þis passage
> I*n*-to þe blis þat eu*e*re schal be,
> 96   Whanne we be*n* passid o*ur*e oolde age.

and pass over death to everlasting bliss.

[" Bothe ȝonge & olde," or " Se what oure lord suffride for oure sake," printed above, pp. 32-4, follows here.]

This World is but a Vanyte.

AN OLD MAN'S LAMENT.

[*Lambeth MS.* 853, *ab.* 1430, A.D., *page* 58 ;
written without breaks.]

	As Y gan wandre in my walkinge	In my walk
	Bisidis an holt vndir an hille,	
	Y say an oolde man sitte wepinge :	I saw an old man sighing, and he said, "Once I had all the world at my will, but now it's all turned to ill.
4	With siȝynge sore he seide me tille,	
	¶ "Sumtime y hadde þe world at wille,	
	With ricchesse & with rialte,	
	And now it is turned al to ille ;	
8	þe worlde is but a vanyte.	
	My silf I likne vnto þe morewe :	I am like the Morning. At my birth my Mother groaned with pain.
	Whanne y was child, & bor[e]n bare,	
	Mi modir for me suffride sorewe	
12	With gruntyngis gril & siȝinge sare;	
	¶ On me was neiþer wem ne hore ;	I was spotless,
	But siþen in synne y haue be ;	
	Now y am oolde y wepe þerfore ;	but now am sinful.
16	þis world is but a vanyte.	
	At mydmore y lerned to go,	At Mid-morn I played, [¹ Page 59.] and like a boy fought.
	And plaied as children doon in ¹strete ;	
	þe kinde of childhode y dide also,	
20	Wiþ my felawis to fiȝte and prete.	
	¶ Al þat y dide, it þouȝte me swete,	All I did, seemed sweet: but now I weep for it. This world is but vanity.
	ffor al þis childhode tauȝte me ;	
	Now y am oolde, þerfore y wepe ;	
24	þis worlde is but a vanite.	

6 *

At Undern 9 A.M.) I was put to school,	**A**t vndre*n* to scole y was sett
	To lerne lore, as oþir dooþ ;
	Whan*n*e my maistir wolde me bet,
and cursed my master when he beat me.	28 I wolde him curse, y w*as* ful wrooþ.
I cared only for joy and jollity,	¶ To lerne good y was ful looþ,
	I þouȝte on ioie & ioilite ;
	Now certis, for to seie þe sooþ,
alas !	32 þis world is b*ut* a vanyte.
At Mid-day I was knighted,	**A**t mydday y was dubbid knyȝt,
	In route y lerned for to ryde ;
and none durst stand my charge.	Was þer noon so hardi a wiȝt
	36 þat in bataile durste me abide.
Where is now my bravery? Not to be hidden from death.	¶ Whe*r*e is bicome now al my pride,
	Mi booldnes, & my fair bewte ?
	Now from deeþ may y me not hide ;
	40 þis world is b*ut* a vanyte.
At High Noon I was crowned King, and fulfilled all my lusts. [¹ Page 60.]	**A**t hiȝ noo*n* y was crowned king,
	þis world was oonli at my wille ;
	Eue*r*e to ¹lyue was my liking,
	44 And alle my lustis to fulfille.
Now age has crept on me.	¶ Now age is cropen on me ful stille,
	A*nd* makiþ me oold & blac of ble,
This world is but vanity.	And y go downeward wiþ þe hille ;
	48 þis World is but a vanite.
At Mid-afternoon my pleasures passed away.	**A**t mydoue*r*noon y droupid faste,
	Mi lust & liking wente away ;
	From iolite myn hert is paste,
	52 From rialte & riche aray.
Man's life here is but a day compared to everlasting life.	¶ Ma*n*nis lijf here is but a day
	Aȝens þe lijf þat eue*r*e schal be ;
	A*nd* oo þing y dare weel say.
	56 þat þis world is but a vanyte.

THIS WORLD IS BUT VANYTE.

  At euensong tyme y wax ful coold,   *At Even Song I*
   And biga𝑛 to go bi staue ;   *walked with a*
  Now is deeþ on me ful boold,   *staff. Death seeks*
60 *And* fo𝑟 his rent he wole me craue.   *me.*
  ¶ Whanne y am deed & leid in graue,   *In the grave*
   þer is no þing þa𝑛𝑛e þat saueþ me   *nought saves but*
  But good or yuel þat y do haue ;   *good done.*
64 þis world is but a vanite.

  Thus is þe day come to nyȝt,   *At Night I loathe*
   þat me loþith of my lyuynge,   *my life. Death*
  And doolful deeþ to me is diȝt,   *and the Grave*
              possess me.
68 *And* i𝑛 coold ¹clay now schal y clinge."   [¹ Page 61.]
  ¶ þus an oold man y herde mornynge
   Biside an holte vndir a tree.   *God grant us His*
  God grau𝑛te us his blis eue𝑟lastinge !   *bliss! for this*
72 þis world is bu𝑡 a vanite.   *world is but vanity.*

[" In a noon tijd," or " *Reuertere*," pp. 91-4 of this volume, follows here in the MS.]

This World is False and Vain.

[*Lambeth MS.* 853, *page* 32, *written without breaks.*]

<table>
<tr><td>Why is this world beloved?</td><td>Whi is þis world biloued þat fals is & veyn,
Siþen þat hise welþis ben so unserteyn?</td></tr>
<tr><td>Its power passes away like a brittle pot.</td><td>¶ Al so soone hee passiþ his power away
4 As dooþ a brokil poot þat freisch is and gay.</td></tr>
<tr><td></td><td>¶ Truste ȝe raþer to lettris written wiþinne þis
þan to þis wrecchid world þat ful of synne is.</td></tr>
<tr><td>It is false in all, and so unstable,</td><td>¶ It is fals in his biheeste, & riȝt disceyuable;
8 It haþ bigilid many a man, it is so vnstable.</td></tr>
<tr><td>[¹ Page 33.]</td><td>¶ It is raþir ¹ to bileeue þe wageringe wijnde
þan þe chaungeable world þat makiþ men so blinde.</td></tr>
<tr><td>false in its business and its pleasures too.</td><td>¶ For wheþer þou slepe or wake, þou schalt fynde it fals
12 Bothe in hise bisinessis & in hise lustis als.</td></tr>
<tr><td>Where is Solomon,

or Samson,</td><td>¶ Telle me where is Salamon, sumtyme a king richee,
Or Sampson þe stronge to whom was no mar liche?</td></tr>
<tr><td>Absalom or Jonathan,</td><td>¶ Or þe fair man absolon, merueilose in cheere,
16 Or þe duke ionatas, a weel biloued fere?</td></tr>
<tr><td>Cæsar

or Dives,</td><td>¶ Where is bicome cesar, þat lorde was of al,
Or þe riche man cloþid in purpur & in pal?</td></tr>
<tr><td>Tully

or Aristotle,</td><td>¶ Telle me where ys tullius, in eloquence so sweete,
20 Or aristotil þe Filosofre wiþ his witt so greete?</td></tr>
</table>

¶ Where ben þese worþi þat were heere-to-forn ?   *or all former*
   Boþe kingis & bischopis, her power is al lorn.   *kings ? All their power is lost,*

¶ Alle þese greete princis with her power so hiȝe   *all vanished in*
24 Ben vanischid now a-way in twynkeling¹ of an yȝe.   *the twinkling of an eye.*
                                                             [1 Page 34.]

¶ Þe ioie of þis wrecchid world is a schoorte feeste,   *This world's joy*
   And it is likened to a schadewe þat may not longe   *is a passing shadow,*
    leste,

¶ And ȝit it drawiþ man from heuen riche blis,   *and yet makes man lose heaven.*
28 And ofte tyme it makiþ him to synne & do a-mys.

¶ Calle no þing þine owne, þerfore, þat þou maist   *Call nothing here thine own;*
    heere leese ;
   For þat þe world haþ lent þee, efte he wole it cese.

¶ Sette þin herte in heuene a-boue, & þenke what   *set thy heart on heaven above.*
    ioie is þere,
32 And þus to dispise þe world y rede þat þou lere.

¶ Þou þat art but wormes meete, poudre, & dust,   *Thou food for worms, exalt not*
   To enhaunce þi silfe in pride sett not þi lust.   *thyself in pride;*

¶ For þou woost not to-day þat þou schalt lyue to-   *thou may'st die to-morrow.*
    morowe,
36 Þerfore do þou euere weel, And þanne schalt þou   *Therefore do well.*
    not sorowe.

¶ It were ful ioieful & sweete, lordschipe to haue,   *Lordship would be good if it could*
   If so þat lordschip miȝte a man fro ²deeþ saue,   *save a man,*
                                                   [2 Page 35.]

¶ But for as myche as a man schal deie at þe laste,   *but it is no honour, only a*
40 It is noo worschip, but a charge, lordschip to   *burden.*
    taaste.

       Omnia terrena   *All earthly things are another's by*
       Per vices sunt aliena :   *turns,*
       nescio sunt cuius ;   *now mine,*
44   **mea nunc, cras huius et huius.**   *now another's.*
       Dic, homo, quid spores,   *What do you hope for, if you cleave*
       si mundo totus adheres ;   *wholly to this world?*
       nulla tecum feres,   *You can take nothing out of it*
48   **licet tu solus haberes.**   *but yourself.*

Earth.

Whanne liif is moost loued, and deeþ is moost hatid:
þanne dooþ deeþ drawe his drawȝt, and makiþ man
ful nakid.
De terra plasmasti me, &c.

Man, made of earth, has only cared how he may be set high up on earth.

ERþe out of erþe is wondirly wrouȝt,
Erþe of erþe haþ gete a dignyte of nouȝt,
Erþe upon erþe haþ sett al his þouȝt,
4 How þat erþe upon erþe may be hiȝ brouȝt.

Man would be a king on earth; but when earth [¹ Page 86.] bids him home, he shall find it hard to part.

¶ Erþe upon erþe wold be a king;
But how erþe schal to erþe, þenkiþ he no ¹ þing;
Whanne þat erþe biddiþ erþe hise rentis hom
  bring,
8 þan schal erþe out of erþe haue a piteuous parting.

Man wins on earth castles, and says 'It is ours.' But he shall suffer sharply for it.

¶ Erþe vpon erþe wynneþ castels & touris,
þan seiþ erþe to erþe 'now is þis al houris:'
Whanne erþe upon erþe haþ biggid up hise
  boure[s],
12 þanne schal erþe upon erþe suffir scharpe schouris.

Man goes on earth glittering in gold, and yet he shall return to earth before he likes.

¶ Erþe gooþ vpon erþe as molde upon molde,
So gooþ erþe upon erþe al gliteringe in golde,
Like as erþe vnto erþe neuere go schulde;
16 And ȝit schal erþe vn-to erþe raþer þan he wolde.

Wretched man, who toilest

¶ O þou wrecchid erþe þat on erþe traueilist nyȝt
  and day

To florische þe erþe, to peynte þe erþe with wan- *to adorn thee with fine raiment,*
   towne aray ;
ȝit schal þou, erþe, for al þi erþe, make þou it *yet shalt thou*
   neuere so queynte & gay,
20 Out of þis erþe into þe erþe, þere to clinge as a *return to earth like a clod.*
   clot of clay.

¶ O wrecchid man, whi art þou proud ¹þat art of [¹ Page 37.] *Why art thou proud who art*
   þe erþe makid ?
Hider brouȝttist þou no schroud, But poore come *made of earth ? Thou camest to*
   þou, and nakid ; *earth naked, and*
Whanne þi soule is went out, & þi bodi in erþe *when thou art*
   rakid, *put in earth, all*
24 Þan þi bodi þat was rank & Vndeuout, Of alle *men will hate thee.*
   men is bihatid.

¶ Out of þis erþe cam to þis erþe þis wrecchid *Thy clothing came from earth*
   garnement ;
To hide þis erþe, to happe þis erþe, to him was *to enwrap thy earth,*
   cloþinge lente ;
Now gooþ erþe upon erþe, ruli, raggid, and rent, *which under the*
28 Þerfore schal erþe vndir þe erþe haue hidiose *earth shall have torment.*
   turment.

¶ Whi þat erþe to myche loueþ erþe, wondir me *Why earth(man) loves earth too*
   þink, *much, I wonder,*
Or whi þat erþe for superflue erþe to sore sweete
   wole or swynk ;
For whanne þat erþe upon erþe is brouȝt with- *for when man comes to the*
   inne þe brink, *grave's brink he shall have a sad*
32 Þan schal erþe of þe erþe haue a rewful swynk. *time of it.*

¶ Lo, erþe upon erþe, considere þou may *Man, thou camest into earth naked,*
   How erþe comeþ into erþe nakid al way,
¶ Whi schulde erþe upon erþe go now so stoute or [Page 38.]
   gay

and shall be so when thou diest.

36 Whanne erþe schal passe out of erþe in so poore aray?

Think on this, and of the judgment at thy resurrection,

¶ Wolde god, þerfore, þis erþe, While þat he is
    upon þis erþe, Vpon þis wolde hertile þinke,
And how þe erþe out of þe erthe schal haue his
    aȝen-risynge,
And þis erþe for þis erþe schal ȝeelde streite
    rekenyng;

and then never for this earth shalt thou displease God.

40 Schulde neuere þan þis erþe for þis erþe myspleso
    heuene king.

Pray therefore,

¶ þerfore, þou erþe, vpon erþe þat so wickidli hast
    wrouȝt,
While þat þou, erþe, art upon erþe, turne aȝen þi
    þouȝt,

man, to God,

And praie to þat god upon erþe þat al þe erþe
    haþ wrouȝt,

that thou may'st come to bliss.

44 þat þou, erþe upon erþe, to blis may be brouȝt.

Lord, let not man come to grief for this earth, but

¶ O þou lord þat madist þis erþe for þis erþe, &
    suffridist heere peynes ille,
Lete neuere þis erþe for þis erþe myscheue ne
    spille,

[¹ Page 88.] here ever work thy will, that he may ascend to thy high hill.

But þat þis erþe on þis ¹erþe be euere worchinge
    þi wille,
48 So þat þis erþe from þis erþe may stie up to þin
    hiȝ hille.   A-M-E-N.

[See an earlier Poem on *Earth*, in alternate English and Latin stanzas, in my edition of *Early English Poems* for the Philological Society, 1862, p. 150-2; and in *Reliquiæ Antiquæ*, vol. ii. p. 216.

Memento homo quod cinis es, and the Creed (pp. 101-3 of this Text), follow here in the MS.

Reuertere!

(in englisch tunge, turne aӡen!)

[*Lambeth MS.* 853, *ab.* 1430 A.D., *page* 61, *written without breaks.*]

  IN a noon tijd of a somer*s* day
    þe su*n*ne schoon ful myrie þat tide,
  I took myn hauk al for to play,
4 Mi spaynel re*n*ny*n*g bi my side.
 ¶ A feisau*n*t hen soone gan y se,
    Myn hou*n*d put up ful fair to fliӡt,
  I sente my fauku*n*, y leet hi*m* flee :
8 It was to me a deinteuose siӡt.

 ¶ My faukun fliӡ faste to his pray,
    I ran þo w*ith* a ful glad chere,
  I spurned ful soone on my way,
12 Mi leg was hent al w*ith* a brere.
 ¶ þis brere forsoþe dide me grijf,
    And soone it made me to tu*r*ne aӡe,
  For he bare written in euer*y* leef
16 þis word in latyn, reuertere.

  I knelid & pullid þe brere me fro,
    A*nd* redde þis word ful hendeli ;
  Myn herte fil dou*n* vnto my too
20 þat was woont sitten ful likingly.
 ¶ I leete myn hauke & feysau*n*t fare,
    Mi spaynel fil dou*n* to my knee,

One sunny summer noon I took out my hawk and spaniel.

The dog put up a hen pheasant, and I flew my falcon at her—a pretty sight.

I ran on fast,

but a briar brought me to grief, and made me turn back, for on every leaf it was written Revertere.

I disentangled myself.

My heart fell to my toe. [Page 62.]

I let the hawk and hen fly,

and sighed over this *Revertere*.	þanne took y me wiþ siȝynge sare
	24 þis new lessoun, reuertere.
It means 'turn again, or back.'	**R**euertere is as myche to say
	In englisch tunge as, turne aȝen :
Turn, then, man and think of thy life, open and hidden.	Turne aȝen, man, y þee pray,
	28 And þinke hertili what þou hast ben ;
	¶ Of þi liuynge be-þinke þee rijfe,
If thou would'st go to heaven, think of '*turn again*.'	In open & in priuite.
	þat þou may come to euerlastinge lijf,
	32 Take to þi mynde reuertere.
I became serious,	**Þ**is word made me to studie sore,
	And binam me al my list ;
and thought how I had spent my life.	How y hadde ledde my lijf so ȝore,
	36 I putt it freischli in-to my brist.
I found myself full far from God,	¶ þanne foond y me ful fer y-flet
	Al from god in maieste ;
	Forsoþe þere schal no þing me leett
and will repent.	40 þat y ne wole synge reuertere.
This summer-noon heat	**T**his noon hete of þe someris day,
[¹ Page 63.]	Whanne þe sunne moost ¹ hiȝest is,
is like	It may be likened in good fay,
	44 For gregorie witnessiþ weel þis ;
	¶ For in ȝonge age men wide doon walke
man in youth, rushing into all kinds of sin.	To dyuers synnis in fele degre :
	þouȝ a ȝong man make a balke,
	48 ȝit take to þi mynde reuertere.
Lust blinds many a man,	**F**or likinge blindiþ many oon
	þat he seeþ not him-silf y-wis,
	And makiþ his herte as hard as stoon ;
and prevents him thinking of heaven.	52 þanne þenkiþ he not on heuen blis ;
	¶ For danyel preueþ it weel riȝtfulli,
	As susannis storie telliþ me,

Two preestis were deemed worþili ;
56   For likinge þei knew not reuertere.

    ȝouþe beriþ þe hauke upon his hond
      Whanne ioilite forȝetiþ age :
    This hauke is mannis herte, y vndirstonde,
60   For it is ȝong & of hiȝ romage.
¶ He puttiþ his hauke fro his fist,
    He þat schulde to god be free ;
    He meltiþ and wexiþ a weel poore gist
64   Whanne ¹he comeþ to reuertere.

    For ful of corage is ȝougeþe in herte,
      And waitynge euere on his pray,
    He ne spariþ ryuer ne þornes smerte
68   To gete his myrþe þere he beest may.
¶ He þat enserchiþ þe derknes of nyȝt,
    And þe myst of þe morowtide may se,
    He schal know bi cristis myȝt
72   If ȝouþe kunne synge reuertere.

    This hauk of herte in ȝouþe y-wys,
      Pursueþ euere þis feisaunt hen ;
    Þis feisaunt hen is likingnes,
76   And euere folewiþ hir þese ȝonge men.
¶ Þis is likinge in euery synne,
    Venial & deedli wheþer it be,
    With greet likinge he wole bigynne,
80   But sorewe bringe forþ reuertere.

    Liking is modir of synnis alle,
      And norischiþ euery wickid dede,
    In foole myscheues sche makiþ to falle,
84   Of al sorowe sche dooþ þe daunce leede.
¶ Þis herte of ȝouþe is hie ¹ of port,
    And wildenes makiþ him ofte to fle,

Youth bears the hawk on his hand.

The hawk is man's heart, and

is flown from the fist, but not to God.

[¹ Page 64.]

Youth watches ever its prey, and

spares no prick of thorn to get its pleasure.

Let the watcher of the night ask whether youth will heed the call 'Turn again.'

This hawk, man's heart, pursues ever the hen pheasant Pleasure.

Lust or Desire is the beginning of every sin,

their mother, and nourisher,

and of all sorrow leads the dance.
[¹ MS. his.]
[Page 65.]
Youth, through wildness,

often goes wrong. Then it should *turn again.*	And ofte to falle in wickid sort; 88 þanne is it þe beste, reuertere.
In pleasure, think that youth must leave thee.	**B**ut be waar of welþe or þou be woo; In iolite whan þou art piȝt, þinke þat ȝonge wole go þe fro, 92 Be þou neuere so greet of miȝt.
When age takes thee, thou wilt think it best to *turn again.*	Whanne age haþ take þee bi þe brest, And for febilnes þou myȝt not se, þin herte seiþ þanne þat it is best 96 For to seie & synge reuertere.
Holy Writ says that a request too long delayed will be refused.	**B**ut in holi writt we fynde If þou þi lord schulde ouȝt aske a þing, For þi longe beinge bihinde, 100 Aȝenseid art þou of þin askinge.
In youth thou didst wild outrage and forgattest *Revertere.*	¶ While þou were ȝonge, in tendre age, Of þin askinge þou were ful free In ydilnes & wilde outrage; 104 þanne was forȝete reuertere.
Let every one think how short a time he shall be here. [¹ Page 66.]	**Þ**erfore euery man biþinke him weel How litil while is his dwellynge; As holy writt yt dooþ telle, 108 He schal not ¹ knowe withoute lesinge.
Cocks crow when midnight comes. Man knows not his time if he cannot say *Revertere.*	¶ A cok can crowe his tyme mydnyȝt, Which he knowith weel in his degre: But his tyme he knowith not ariȝt 112 þat can weel neuere seie reuertere.
Think, then, man, that there is no so poor wretch as thou.	**T**herfore be þou in certein, man, While þou muste knowe how; Biþinke þi silf how þou art þan; 116 Noon so poore a wrecche as þou!
Pray we all to God to grant everlasting bliss to all who can say '*Turn again.*'	¶ þerfore praye we to heuene king, Euery man in his degree, To graunte them þe blis euerlastinge 120 þat þis word weel kan seie, reuertere.

Merci Passiþ Riȝtwisnes.

(A DIALOGUE BETWEEN A SINNER AND MERCY.)

[*Lambeth MS.* 853, *ab.* 1430 A.D., *pages* 66 *to* 73; *written without breaks.*]

BI a forest as y gan walke
    Wiþ-out a paleys in a leye,
    I herde two men togidre talke ;
4   I þouȝte to wite what þei wolde seie.
¶ Þat oon stood in a doolful aray,
    Hise deedli synnis he gan to defie,
    "Alas," he seide, me dreediþ to-day
8   Þat riȝt wole forþ, & no mercye."

¶ Þanne answeride merci wiþ sobir ¹cheer,
    " Man, me þinkiþ þi witt is bare ;
    If þou wolt, y schal þee leer,
12   Þee nediþ not to moorne so sare.
¶ I rede þee to foonde to ameende þi fare ;
    Go euery day & heere a messe,
    And schryue þee cleene, & haue noo care,
16   For mercy passiþ riȝtwisnes."

¶ Þanne seide þe synner wiþ angri mood,
    " Man, me þenkist² þou docst raue ;
    I woot weel þou canst no good,
20   Þou barist neuere staat but as a knawe.

As I walked I heard two men talking.

One was very sad, fearing that Right would be done, without Mercy.

[¹ Page 67]
But Mercy said, Man, you need not mourn.

Amend your ways, hear Mass daily, be shriven, and fear not, Mercy passeth Righteousness.

The Sinner answered, Thou ravest :
[² *for* þenkiþ]

as I deserve, so shall I haue;		¶ As y deserue, so schal y haue; Weel bittirli y schal a-bie; I knowe noon helpe þat me schulde haue,
Right, not Mercy.	24	But þat riȝt schal forþ, and no mercie."
Mercy. If thou wilt give up thy sin,		¶ Þanne seide mercye meeke & mylde, "If þou wolt fro þi synnes drawe, Þouȝ þou speke þese wordis wilde,
	28	To helpe þee ȝit I wolde be fawe.
love God and repent, [¹ Page 68.] He is over the law: His Mercy exceeds His Justice.		¶ Loue weel god, þat is my sawe, Repente þee blyue of ¹ al þi mys; Almyȝti god is ouer þe lawe,
	32	His merci passiþ his riȝtwisnes."
The Sinner. [² or fonoued.]		"Seie me," quod þe synner, "þou fooуued ² clerk. Þou coudist neuere rede in no spel;
I never willingly did a good deed;	36	I wrouȝte wilfulli neuere good werk; What riȝt haue y in heuen to dwelle?
I deserve hell;		¶ I haue deserued to go to helle, And þerfore ofte sore sike y;
my wicked deeds will kill me. Right, and no Mercy, on me.	40	My wickid dedis wole me quelle, Þere riȝt schal forþ, and no mercye."
Mercy. God shed His blood for thee and me,		¶ Merci seide "þou canst no good; God schewiþ þee kyndenes many foolde, For þee & me he schedde his blood,
	44	And suffride woundis bittir & colde.
and bought us with his flesh.		¶ His fair body to þe iewis was solde To bie oure synful soulis to blis;
Thy soul is His. He will have mercy.	48	Þi soule is his, y myȝt be bolde; His merci passiþ his ryȝtwisnes."
The Sinner. I know God is good and true, and loves Truth.		¶ "Forsoþe," quod þe synner, "þat leue y weel, Þat he is boþe good & kynde, And þerto trewer þan ony steel;
	52	Þat he loueþ truþe weel schal y fynde.

¶ How my3t god me of care vnbinde
    Siþen god loueþ trouþe so verrili?
    Do way, mercy, þou spillist myche winde,
56   For ri3t schal forþ, & no mercy."

    [Page 69.] How then shall He free me? Right will prevail, not Mercy.

¶ Merci seide, "woldist þou god knowe,
    And wiþ good entent mercy calle,
    And to him meekeli þee abowe,
60   þan schal neuere myscheef in þee falle.
¶ þou3 þou haddist do þe synnis alle,
    And þou crie mercy for al þi mys,
    And with good herte on him to calle,
64   þan wole his mercy passe ri3twisnes."

Mercy. If thou wilt really pray for mercy, though thou hast sinned all the sins, God's Mercy will exceed His Justice.

¶ "What," quod þe synner, "y trowe þou raue;
    Canst þou neuere of þi pletinge blynne?
    þe deuel bad ne neuere mercy craue,
68   And he can more clergie þan al þi kynne;
¶ And he him silf is ful of synne,
    And 3it wole he neuere mercy crie:
    I coueite neuere heuen to wynne
72   While ri3t schal forþ, & no mercie."

The Sinner. Nonsense! The Devil bad me never ask mercy; and he knows more than thou. He is full of sin, and never asks mercy; Justice will prevail.

¶ Merci seide " y preue bi skile,
    Witt is nou3t worþ, but grace be sou3t;
    þe deuel ¹Haþ clergie & witt at wille,
76   And euere he settiþ it foule at nou3t:
¶ He fil in wanhope as him neuere rou3te,
    þoru3 pride in heuen he loste his blis;
    Hadde he oonys grace bisou3te,
80   Merci hadde passid ri3twijsnes."

Mercy. The devil's wit is no good without grace. [¹ Page 70.] He fell into despair when he lost heaven. Had he sought grace he'd have had Mercy.

¶ Whanne þe synner herd þis, he si3ed sore,
    With rewful cheer greet dool he made,
    And seide, "of þee wole y lerne more;
84   þan is the deuel fals and bad,
¶ For if he my3te merci haue had,

The Sinner. I'll learn of thee. The devil must be bad if he might have had mercy.

MERCI PASSITH RIƷTWISNESS.

*He needs be sorry who gets Right and not Mercy.
MS. transposes riȝtwisnes and mercy.]*

  A þousand siþis y him defie ;
  He may be sory & no-þing glad
88 þat schal haue ¹riȝtwisnes & no mercy."

Mercy.

Dear brother, give up the devil, who would send you to hell.

Pray for grace, God will send it, and thy soul will go to heaven.

Mercy biheeld þat semeli goost,
  And seide, " leue broþer, forsake þe feend,
  For he wolde fayn þi soule were lost,
92 To dwelle in helle without eend.
 ¶ Bisecho now grace, & god wole sende
  And þou wolt do as y þee wijs,
  And þan þi soule to heuen schal wende,
96 þere merci passiþ riȝtwisnes."

*The Sinner.
[Page 71.]
My past life is worthless;
I will serve God; may He keep me from sin.*

I defy the false fiend who promised me Right, not Mercy.

"**A**las," quod þe synner, " al my lijf y rue,
  For it is no þing as y wende ;
  To serue god y wole be trewe
100 If ony grace he wole me sende.
 ¶ Of al wickidnes he me defende !
  þe fals feend, y him defie ;
  He wolde no þing þat y dide meende,
104 þat biheet me riȝt & no mercie."

Mcrey.

Do so, and rejoice. Be sorry for thy sin, be shriven, do

penance, and

repent: Thou shalt know that Mercy passes Justice.

Merci seide " if þou wolt so,
  þou myȝt be glad al þi lijf,
  And for þi synne þou maist be woo,
108 And to a preest cleene þee schriue,
 ¶ And take penaunce without strijf,
  Repentynge þee of al þi mys,
  þan bi þi witt þou maist knowe rijf
112 þat merci passiþ riȝtwisnes."

The Sinner.

No penaunce is enough for me: not being buried alive.

"**A**las," quod the synner, y haue lyued wrong !
  What penaunce were y worþi to haue ?
  þer may no man sette me to strong
116 þouȝ y were quicke doluen on graue.

¶ A! almiȝty god, mercy I craue,
　　Now lete my flesche my synnis abie!
　Graciose crist! my soule þou haue,
120　For riȝt is nouȝt wiþout mercie."

Ah God! have mercy. Christ, take my soul.

[Page 72.]

Mercy seide, "ful weel þou woost,
　　As þou hast often herd sayen,
　What man is founde þat was lost,
124　Wiþ him is crist plesid & fayn.
　¶ What nede had crist to suffre payne
　　But for to bie oure soulis to blis?
　Telle me þi lijf heere al playn,
128　þat mercy may passe riȝtwisnes."

Mercy.
Christ rejoices over the lost sinner who is found.

Tell me all thy sins.

"**M**y fyue wittis y haue mys spende
　　þoruȝ pride, enuie, & leccherie:
　To þe ten heestis y haue not tende
132　þoruȝ slouþe, wraþþe, & glotenie.
　¶ In coueitise lyued haue y,
　　And neuere dide werkis of mercyes;
　God! ȝeue me grace or þat y die!
136　þi merci may passe riȝtwisnes."

The Sinner.
I have misspent my Five Senses; disobeyed the Ten Commandments; lived in covetousness, and done no good works.

God, let thy Mercy pass thy Justice.

Merci ȝaf him penaunce stronge,
　　And seide "man, wolt þou þis take?
　þou muste suffre boþe riȝt and wrong;
140　If þou þi synne wolt forsake,
　¶ In good praiers þou muste wake,
　　And neuere ¹ wilne to do a-mys;
　And for þi sorewe þat þou doost make,
144　Merci schal passe riȝtwisnes."

Mercy.
Do this penance: Suffer, and forsake thy sin.

Watch and pray.
Never will to sin.
[1 Page 73.]
Then Mercy shall exceed Justice.

Þe synner took penaunce wiþ good entent,
　And lefte al his wickid synne;
　Whanne he hadde leeue, away he went

The sinner forsook his sins,

7 *

and all his friends; did great penance, and no sin wilfully. He trusted to God to bring him to heaven.	148
	
	152
		From alle his freendis, kiþ & kynne.
		¶ In greet penaunce he putte him inne,
		    And neuere aftir wilfulli dide mys;
		He truste on god heuen to wynne,
		    þere mercy passiþ riȝtwijsnes.

Lord! give us grace, and be merciful to us.
 	
Mary, guide our souls to thy Son,
where Mercy prevails over Justice.
	
	156
	
	160
		Almiȝti god! now make us stable,
		    And ȝeue us grace weel to spede,
		And to us alle bee merciable,
		    And forȝeue us alle oure mysdede.
		¶ And helpe us, ladi, att oure moost nede,
		    To þi sone oure soulis þou wys,
		And with his mercy fulli us fede
		    þere mercy passiþ riȝtwijsnes. A-M-E-N.

["As rosoun rewlid," or "Filius Regis Mortuus est," follows.
It is printed in *Political, Religious, and Love Poems*, p. 205, &c.]

The Belief.

[*Lambeth MS.* 853, *ab.* 1430 A.D., *page* 39; *written without breaks.*]

¶ Memento homo quod cinis es, et in cinerem reuerteris. — Remember, man, that thou art dust.
¶ Fac bene dum viuis. Post mortem viuere si uis. — Do well while thou livest.
¶ Tangere qui gaudet. meretricem qualiter audet. Palmis pollutis, regem tractare salutis. — How does he who delights to touch a harlot, dare to handle the King of Salvation with polluted hands.
Credo in deum patrem omnipotentem.

 IN þee, god fadir, I bileeue, — I believe in God the Father,
  þe firste persoone ful of myȝt,
  þat al of nouȝt hast maad to meeue,
4 boþe heuen & erþe, day & nyȝt.

¶ And in þin oonly goten sone, — and in His only begotten Son,
  Born of þi silf bifor al þing,
  Oure lord ihesus, þe secunde persoone, — Jesu Christ, one with God,
8 Bothe oo god in heuen beinge.

¶ Þe same god þat euere haþ ben, — conceived by the Holy Ghost, and born of a pure virgin,
  And siþen conceyued bi þe holi goost,
  And born of a mayden cleene,
12 Bicause a man in meekenes moost. [Page 40.]

¶ And riȝt as in þe trynyte
  Ben persoones þre, substauncis but oon, — (of three substances, God, soul, body)
  Riȝt so in þee ben substauncis þre,
16 God, soule, bodi, & al oon persoone.

THE BELIEF.

who suffered under Pontius Pilate, was crucified,

¶ Undir pilate þou suffridist peyne
  Bi fre wil, mankinde to saue,
  Nailid on a croos, & þeron slain,

and buried,

20 And taken doun & biried in graue.

descended into hell,

¶ In soule oonli þou wente to helle,
  & took þens þi part, it was good riȝt,

but rose again the third day,

But up þou roos in fleisch and in felle
24 þe þrid day bi godli myȝt.

ascended into heaven,

¶ þou stiȝ to heuen in þi manhede,
  And þere þou sittist on þi fadir riȝt side,
  But ouer al-where is þi godhede,
28 þere is noon þat from þee him may hide.

whence He shall come to judge both quick and dead,

¶ þens schalt þou come us alle to deeme,
  Boþe quik and dede of adams seed.
  With opene woundis & visage breme ;
32 þis bileeue makiþ true men drede.

[¹ Page 41.] I believe in the] Holy Ghost,

¶ I bileeue in þe holi ¹goost,
  þe þridde persoone in trynyte,
  Of which þre noon is more ne moost,
36 But al oon god in persoones þre.

who makes Holy Church, by faithful men giving each to other what each can,

¶ þe holi goost makiþ holi chirche
  Of feiþful men, bi comynynge
  Ech oon to oþir what þei kunne worche
40 In holines and good lyuyng.

I believe in the Forgiveness of Sins (through the Sacrament),

¶ Forȝeeuenes y bileeue of synne
  Bi þe holi goost and þe sacrament,
  If y maye goostli to hem wynne,
44 Or ellis him silfe is euere present.

¶ þouȝ he neuere so present be,
  Ȝit he wole for ful meekenes

þat y do þerto þat is in me,
48   Lest contempt lette me of forȝeuenes.

¶ Also y bileeue in hool mynde,   *and that the Holy*
    þe holi goost schalle knytte aȝen   *Ghost shall knit again all men's*
    þe soule to þe fleische of al mankinde ;   *souls to their flesh on their*
52   For al fleish schal ryse þat deeþ hath slayn.   *resurrection,*

¶ þe holi goost schal ȝeue also   *and shall give*
    Euerlastynge lijf to alle true men.   *everlasting life to all true men.*
    þat we may heere serue þer-to,
56   ¶ Y rede we seie alle, amen.

[*The Sixteen Points of Charity*, or "Man, among þi myrþis,"
printed p. 114, below, follows here in the MS.]

The Ten Commandments.

[*Lambeth MS.* 1853, *ab.* 430 A.D., *page* 47 ; *written without breaks.*]

<small>Every one should teach his children these, and keep them himself.</small>

EUery man schulde teche þis lore
    To hise children wiþ good entent,
And do it him-silf euermore,
4   To kepe weel goddis comaundement.

<small>I. Have no false gods. Worship God Almighty.</small>

¶ Fals goddis þou schalt noon haue,
    But worschipe god omnipotent ;
Make not þi god þat man haþ graue :
8   þis is þe firste comaundement.

<small>II. Take not God's name in vain. Swear by no created thing.</small>

¶ Goddis name in ydil take þou not,
    For if þou do þou schalt be scheent ;
Swere bi no þing þat god haþ wrouȝt :
12   þis is þe secunde comaundement.

<small>III. Hallow the Holy Day.</small>

¶ Haue mynde to helewe þin holi day,
    þou & alle þine wiþ good entent ;
Leue seruile werkis & nyce aray :
16   þis is þe þridde comaundement.

<small>IV. Honour thy Father and Mother.

[¹ Page 41.]</small>

¶ Worschipe þi fadir & þi modir boþe,—
    þat longe lijf to þee be lent,—
Wiþ meete ¹and drink, coumfort & cloþe :
20   þis is þe iiijᵉ comaundement.

<small>V. Kill no man,</small>

¶ Sle no man wiþ yuel wille,
    Ensaumple, or tunge, or strokis dent ;

	But euermore do good for ille :	but do good for ill.
24	þis is þe fifthe comaundement.	

	¶ Do no leccherie in al þi lijf ;	VI. Commit not adultery or fornication.
	Lete fleischeli knowynge from þee be lent	
	Saue oonli bi-twene man & wijf :	
28	þis is þe sixte comaundement.	

	¶ þou schalt not stele no maner of þing,	VII. Steal not.
	Ne helpe þerto bi no consent.	
	Leue alle fals mesuris & al gilinge :	Use no deceit.
32	þis is þe .vij. comaundement.	

	¶ þou schalt beere no fals witnes	VIII. Bear no false witness,
	For no mater þat may be ment ;	
	Seie euere þe soþe, or holde þi pees :	
36	þis is þe .viij. comaundement.	

	¶ þou schalt not coueite þi neiʒboris good,	IX. Covet not thy neighbour's goods.
	As hous, lond, catel, ne rent,	
	In hindringe of him & of his blood :	
40	þis is þe .ix. comaundement.	

	¶ þou schalt not desire þi neiʒboris feere,	X. Covet not thy neighbour's wife; take not his servant or goods falsely. [1 Page 49.]
	Ne falsli his seruaunt from him hent,	
	Ne no good þat [1] he hath heere :	
44	þis is þe .x. comaundement.	

	¶ þese ten to kepe, þou ʒeue us grace	Christ, give us grace to keep these Ten
	þat on þe roode was al to-rent,	
	In-to his blis þat we mowe passe	that we may pass to bliss.
48	At þe laste day of Iugement.	

["I Warne eche lijf," p. 107, &c., of this print, followe here in the MS.]

Kepe Wel Cristes Comaundement.

[*Vernon MS.*, *ab.* 1370 A.D., *fol.* 408 *b.*, *col.* 1.
Printed here for comparison' sake, with the metrical
points, but no stops.]

    I warne vche leod. þat liueþ in londe.
    And do hem dredles. out of were.
    Þat þei most studie. and vnderstonde.
4 Þe lawe of crist. to loue and lere.
    Þer nis no mon. fer ne nere.
    Þat may him seluen. saue vn-schent.
    But he þat casteþ. wiþ concience clere.
8 To kepe. wel. Cristes Comaundement.

    Þow most haue o God. and no mo.
    And serue him boþe. with mayn and miht.
    And ouer alle þinges. loue him also.
12 For he haþ lant þe. lyf and liht.
    ȝif þou beo nuyȝed. day or niht.
    In peyne be meke. and pacient.
    And rule þe ay. be reson riht.
16 And kep wel. Cristes Comaundement.

    ¶ And let þi neiȝhebor. frend and fo.
    Riht frely. of þi frendschupe fele.
    In herte. þat þou wilne hem so.
20 Riht as þou woldest. þi self weore wele.
    And help to sauen hem. from vncele.
    So þat heore soules. beo not schent.
    And also heore care. þou helpe to kele.
24 And kepe wel. Cristes comaundement.

Kepe Weel Cristis Comaundement.

[*Lambeth MS.* 853, *ab.* 1430 A.D., *page* 49; *written without breaks.*]

I Warne eche lijf þat liueþ in lond   *Every man must take care to love*
 And do him dredlees out of were,   *the Law of God.*
þat he must studie & vndirstonde
4 þe lawe of god to loue & lere.
¶ For þere is no man feer ne neer   *Only he can be saved who gives*
 þat may him sillfe saue vnschent   *himself to keep Christ's*
But he þat castiþ him with conscience clere *Commandments.*
8 To kepe weel cristis comaundement.

Thou schalt haue oon god & no mo,   *I. Thou shalt have one God,*
 And serue him boþe wiþ mayn & myȝt,
And ouer al þing loue him also,   *and love Him above every-*
12 For he haþ lent þee lijf & liȝt.   *thing.*
¶ If þou be noied bi day or nyȝt,
 In peyne be meeke & pacient,   *Be patient in suffering.*
And rewle þee ay bi resoun riȝt,
16 And kepe weel cristis comaundement.

Lete þi neiȝe-¹boris, boþe freend & fo,   [¹ Page 50.]
 Freli of þi freendschip feele;   *Love thy neighbour as*
In herte wilne þou hem also   *thyself;*
20 Riȝt as þou woldist þi silf were wele.
¶ Helpe to saue hem from vnsele   *and help to save*
 So þat her soulis ben not schent,   *him from all ill.*
And her care þou helpe to kele,
24 And kepe weel cristis comaundement.

¶ In Idel. Godes nome tak þou nouȝt.
But cese. and saue þe from þat synne.
Swere bi no þing. þat God haþ wrouht.
28 Be war. his wraþþe. lest þou hit wynne.
But bisy þe her. bale to blynne.
þat blaberyng are wiþ oþes blent.
Vncouþe *and* knowen. *and* of þi kynne.
32 And kep wel. cristes comaundement.

¶ In clannes and in cristes werk.
Haue mynde. to holden þin haly day.
And drauh þe þenne. from dedes derk.
36 Wiþ al þi meyne. Mon and may.
And men vnsauȝte. loke þou assay.
To sauȝten hem þenne. at on assent.
And pore and seke. þou plese *and* pay.
40 And kepe wel cristes Comaundement.

¶ þi Fader þi Moder. þou worschupe boþe.
Ȝif þou wolt boteles. bale escheuwe.
With counseil cum-forte hem. with mete *and*
cloþe.
44 As þou sest. hem neodeþ newe.
And ȝif þei talke of tales vn-trewe.
þou torn hem out. of þat entent.
And cristes lawe. help þat þei knewe.
48 And kep wel cristes. Comaundement.

¶ Sle no mon. wiþ wikked wille.
Be war. and vengeaunce tak þou non.
In word. ne dede. loude. ne stille.
52 Bakbyte þou no mon. blod ny bon.
But ay let gabbynges. glyde and gon.
A-wey wher þei wol. glace. or glent.
And help þat alle men ben aton.
56 And kep wel cristes comaundement.

Goddis name in ydil take þou nouȝt,
    But ceesse & saue þee from þat synne;
  Swere bi no þing þat god haþ wrouȝt,
28   Be waar his wraþþe lest þou so wynne.
  ¶ But bisie þee euere her bale to blinne
    þat wiþ blaberinge ooþis ben blent,
  Vncouþe & knowen of þi kynne;
32   And kepe weel cristis comaundement.

II. Take not God's name in vain,
Swear by no thing that God has made,
but keep from the bale of blabbering oath-swearers.

In clennes and in cristis werk
    Haue mynde to halowe þin holi daye,
  And drawe þee þanne from dedis derk
36   Wiþ al þi meyne, man & may.
  ¶ Men vnsoft, loke þou asay
    To soften 'them to good assent,
  Helpe poore and sike to please & pay,
40   And kepe weel cristis comaundement.

III. Hallow thy Holy Day, with all thy household.
Try to soften unsoft men, [1 Page 51.] and to help the poor and sick.

Þi fadir & modir worschipe boþe—
    If þou wolt botelees bale eschewe—
  With councelle, coumforte, meete & cloþe,
44   As þou seest þat hem nediþ newe.
  ¶ And if þei talke of wordis vntrewe,
    þou turne hem out of þat entent,
  And cristis lawe helpe þat þei knew,
48   And kepe weel cristis comaundement.

IV. Honour thy Father and Mother with counsel, food, and clothes.
Turn them from untrue words, and help them to know Christ's law.

Sle no man with wickid wille;
    Be waar, of veniaunce take þou noon;
  Eerli ne late, lowde ne stille,
52   Bacbite no man, blood ne boon,
  ¶ But lete euere gabbing glide & goon
    Away, wheþer it wole glase or glent;
  And helpe þat alle men were at oone,
56   And kepe weel cristis comaundement.

V. Slay no man: take no vengeance.
Backbite no one, but let gabbing go by.
Help on peace.

¶ Stele þou nouȝt. þi neiȝebors þing.
Nouþur wiþ stillenes. ne wiþ strif.
Nor with no maner. wrong getyng.
60 þi self þi seruaunt. child. ne wyf.
To sulle and buye. ȝif þou be ryf.
Wayte al way. þat wrong be went.
As þou wolt lyue. þe lastyng lyf.
64 Þou kepe wel. cristes comaundement.

[Col. 2.]

Fals witnesse. loke þow non bere.
Ȝif þow wolt. in blisse a-byde.
þi neiȝebore. wityngly to dere.
68 Ne no mon nouþer. in no syde.
But loke þat no mon. be a nuyȝed.
And þou may him. from harmes hent.
And help þat falshede. beo distruiet.
72 And kep wel. cristes comaundement.

¶ Sunge þou not. in lecherie.
Such lust vn leueful. let hit pas.
Consente þou not. to such folye.
76 þat founden is so foul trespas.
And loke. þat nouþer more ne las.
þi lykyng. on þat lust be lent.
Leste þou synge. þis songe allas.
80 For brekyng. of cristes comaundement.

¶ þi neiȝhebors wyf. coueyte þou nouȝt.
Vnleuefully. a-ȝeynes þe lawe.
Wiþ hire to sunge. in word ne þouȝt.
84 And from þat deede. euer þou þe drawe.
And neuer sey. to hire no sawe.
To make hire. to synne assent.
Ne plese hire not. with no mis plawe.
88 But kep wel. cristes comaundement.

Synne þou not in leccherie;
Such lust vnleefful, lete it passe;
Consente þou not to þat folie
60 þat founden it is so ¹foule a trespase.
¶ And loke þou, neiþer more ne lasse
þi likinge on þat lust be lent,
Lest þou singe þis song 'alas
64   For brekinge of cristis comaundement.'

VI. Sin not in Lechery and unlawful lust;

[¹ Page 52.] set not thy liking on it

lest thou repent it.

Stele þou nouȝt of þi neiȝboris þing
Neiþer wiþ stilnes ne with strijf,
Ne with no maner of wrong geetynge,
68 þi silf, þi seruaunt, child, ne wijf.
¶ To hie & sille if þou be rijfe,
Loke euere þat wrong away be went:
If þou wolt han euerlastinge lijf,
72   Kepe weel cristis comaundement.

VII. Steal nothing of thy neighbour's.

Cheat not in buying and selling.

Fals witnes, loke þat þou noon bare;
If þou wolt in blis a-bide,
þi neiȝbore wilfulli þou ne dere,
76 Ne noon þat woneþ þee biside;
¶ But loke þat no man be anoied
If þou may him from harmes hent,
And helpe þat falshede were distroied,
80   And kepe weel cristis comaundement.

VIII. Bear no false witness. Injure not thy neighbour, but keep every one from harm. Help to destroy falsehood.

Þi neiȝboris wijf coueite þou nouȝt
Vnleeffulli aȝens þe lawe
Wiþ hir to synne in dede or þouȝt,
84 But from þe dede euere þou drawe,
¶ And ceesse, & seie to hir no sawe
To make hir for to synne assent,
Ne please hir not with no nyce plawe,
88   But kepe weel cristis comaundement.

IX. Covet not thy neighbour's wife, [Page 53.]

and say and do nothing to make her assent to sin.

¶ þi neiȝhebors hous. wenche ne knaue.
Vnskilfully. coueyte þou nouht.
Ne ȝit his good. with wrong to haue.
92 For hit. lest þou to bale be brouht.
For whon þe soþe. schal vp be souht.
Ȝif þou in to þis sunnes assent.
Ful bitterly. hit mot be bouȝt.
96 For brekyng of cristes. Comaundement.

¶ Vche mon þat wol. þis lessun lere.
And loueþ. a laweful lyf. to lede.
He may not misse. on none manere.
100 Þe merþe of heuene. to his mede.
For crist him here. wol helpe and hede.
And heþene. in to heuene hent.
For þi I. preye. þat crist vs spede.
104 Kuyndely to kepe. his comaundement.

Thi neiȝboris hous, wenche, ne knawe,   *Covet not thy neighbour's*
    Vnleeffulli coueite þou nouȝt,   *house, maid, or man,*
  Ne oþir good, wrong to haue,
92   Lest þou for it to bale be brouȝt.
  ¶ For whanne þe sooþe schal be up souȝt,   *for at the Last Day thou shalt*
    If þou to þis synne assent,   *pay bitterly for it.*
  Ful bittirli it schal be bouȝt
96   For brekinge of cristis comaundement.

Ech man þat wole þis lessoun lere,   *No man who learns this lesson*
    And loueþ a lawful lijf to lede,   *can miss the joys of heaven,*
  He ne may mys on no manere
100   þe myrþis of heuen to haue to meede;
  ¶ For crist wole him heere helpe at nede,   *for Christ will take him there.*
    For from hens to heuene be wole him hent,   *Let us pray Him*
  For-þi praie we þat crist us spede   *that we may keep His Command-*
104   Kindeli to kepe his comaundement. Amen.   *ments.*

["There is no creatour but oon," printed pp. 18-21, follows here in the MS.]

The Sixtene Poyntis of Charite.

[*Lambeth MS.* 853, *ab.* 1430 A.D., *page* 42; *written without breaks, except lines* 6-12, 21-4.]

<small>Man, remember whence thou camest, and whither thou goest,</small>

MAn, among þi myrþis haue in mynde
 From whens þou come & whidir þou teendis,
How freelli þou fallist & filist þi kinde !
4 Arise & make of þi mys ameendis,

<small>and that hereafter thou may'st see thy Lord as His chosen child in Charity.</small>

¶ Þat of þis world whanne þou out wendis,
 Þou maist in heuene þi lord god se
Among hise apostolis & dere freendis
8 As 'a chosen child in charitee.

<small>Man's highest task is to live a just life.</small>

The hiȝest lessoun þat man may lere
 Is to lyue iust lijf, if þou wolt loke,
Yf þou haue grace to holde & heere,
12 Is playnli printid in poulis booke.

<small>God told St Paul in the third heaven the 16 points of Charity.</small>

¶ For god to poul þis lessoun tooke
 in þe þridde heuen, hiȝest of þre,
Euery man to cunne & looke
16 Þe sixtene propirtees of charitee.

<small>Though I speak with angels' tongues, and have not Charity, I am but as a brazen cymbal.</small>

'**T**houȝ y speke,' seiþ seint poule,
 'As aungils doon, or with mennis tunge,
If charite be not in þi soule,
20 I am but as a brasen symbal song.

<small>[Page 43.] And though I can move mountains, I am worthless if I want Charity.</small>

¶ And þouȝ my bileeue be neuere so strong
 So þat mounteyns be meued bi feiþ of me,
I am not worthi to god so longe
24 As me wantiþ charite.

  Thouȝ y to poore men ȝeue al my good,
    And my bodi to brenne þere hoot fier ys,
   And charite be not in my mood,
28 It profitiþ me not to heuen blis.'
  ¶ But for god wolde it schulde not mys
    To knowe in charite whanne we be,
    He tauȝte poul to teche al his
32   þe .xvj. Poyntis of charite.

  'Charite,' he seiþ, 'is pacient,
    Alle disesis meekli suffringe,
   Benigne also in hir entent,
36 Kindelid with fier of good lyuyng;
  ¶ Neuere enuyose for ony þing
    To freend ne foo, wheþir it be,
   But euere glad to goddis plesing
40   To cherische alle men in charitee.

  Charite dooþ neuere wickidli
    Bi purpos of wil, ne wickid dede,
   Ne blowen ¹ is with pride þouȝ sche be welþi,
44 For to greue god is hir moost drede ;
  ¶ For in helle depe schal be her meede,
    A low wiþ lucifir for to be
   Þat for blynde pride wole take noon hede
48   lowli to lyue in charite.

  Charite is not coueitose toold
    Of worschipe ne of wronge wynnynge,
   For wiþ ypocritis sche may not holde,
52 Ne consente with wrong getyng.
  ¶ Sche sechiþ not hir owne þing
    for hindringe of neiȝboris þat myȝte be,
   For manye perels ben in pletynge
56   Þat acorden not with charitee.

Side notes:

And though I give my body to be burned, and have not Charity, it profits nothing.

God told Paul to teach his disciples the 16 points of Charity.

1. Charity is patient, and
2. Benign,
3. Never envious,

4. Never does wickedly,
5. Is not puffed up with pride,

¹ [Page 44.]

6. Desires no honour or wrong gains,

7. Seeketh not her own,

8. Is not easily provoked,

Charitee wole no þing be wrooþ
  For harmes þat hir silf may hent,
But for to synne, al oonli is hir looþ,
60   Aȝens goddis comaundement.

9. Thinketh no evil,

¶ Charitee þenkiþ noon yuel in hir entent,
  But stintiþ strijf, & stoondiþ free;
Al yuel wil, it wolde were went,
64   And chaungid al for charite.

[Page 45.]
10. Rejoiceth not in iniquity, but

Of wickidnes charite is not glad,
  Bi lauȝter ne bi no likinge,
But euere sobre, soft, & sad,
68   In þouȝt, in word, & in worching.

11. Rejoiceth in the truth.

¶ To riȝt & troupe is hir ioiyng,
  To maynteine truþe where-euere sche be,
With feiþful and true folk Is hir dwelling,
72   For suche ben chosen in charite.

12. Charity beareth all things,

Alle þingis sche beriþ vp meekeli,
  For al hir wronge schal turne to game;
Sche falliþ not vnder for vilonye,
76   For los, for sijknes, ne for schame.

13. Believeth all things,

¶ Alle þingis sche trowiþ wiþ-out fame
  þat goddis lawe techiþ truþe to be,
And bidiþ þerbi for ony blame,
80   For suche ben children of charitee.

14. Hopeth all things,

Alle þingis sche hopiþ to haue in blis;
  For suche sche suffriþ & seruep heere;
For of mercy sche may not mys
84   þat þis lesson wole loue & lere.

15. Endureth all things.

¶ Sche abidiþ alle þingis with good chere
  þouȝ sche þinke longe þe eende to se,

[¹ Page 46.]

For of reward sche haþ ¹no were
88   þat þus abidiþ in charite.

THE XVI POYNTIS OF CHARITE.

 Charite falliþ neuere a-way   *16. Charity never faileth.*
  From him þat it in charite wole holde,
  Bifore ne aftir domys day,
92   But encresiþ in blis an hundrid folde.
 ¶ Whanne al tresour is tried & tolde,   *All help to bliss is in these three:*
  Al help to blis is in þese þre,   *Faith, hope, charity:*
  Feiþ, hope, & charite, noþing colde ;   *and the greatest of these is*
96   þe mooste of hem is charite.'   *charity.*

 Bi charite, man, þou must loue more   *It makes thee love God above*
  God þan silf, þe sooþ to say,   *thyself,*
  For þis is þe lord-is owne lore,
100   With al þi power him please & pay ;
 ¶ Thi neiȝbore also, wiþ-oute nay,   *and thy neighbour*
  Loue as þi silf saaf to bee ;   *as thyself.*
  To freend & fo holde faste þi fay,
104   And chaunge þou neuere fro charite.

 If we þis lessoun we loue & leere,   *If we learn this lesson, we shall*
  And take it truli to oure entent,   *know who will be blessed and who*
  We schulen haue knowinge good & cleere   *punished.*
108   Who ben blamelees & who ben schent.
  God, þat hast us oure lijf lent,   *God grant that*
  Graunte þat we may oure ¹ silf to enserche   [¹ *Page 47.*]
   & so,
  As þou for us on roode were rent,   *Christ may choose us, for His love.*
112   þou chese us to þee for charite. A-M-E-N.

["Euery man schulde teche þis lore," printed p. 104-5, follows here in the MS.]

Quindecim Signa ante diem Judicij.

[*MS. B.* 11. 24, *Trinity College, Cambridge;
ab.* 1450, A.D.]

<table>
<tr><td>Lord of Heaven,
have mercy on us!</td><td>Kynge of grace, & ful of pyte,
Lord of heuyn, I-blyssyd þou be !
Haue mercy on vs, we the beseche,</td></tr>
</table>

Lord of Heaven, have mercy on us!

    Kynge of grace, & ful of pyte,
    Lord of heuyn, I-blyssyd þou be !
    Haue mercy on vs, we the beseche,
4 Or we lese our wytt & speche !

I will tell of the xv. Signs before Doomsday.

    xv. tokenys telle I may
    That shal come before doomys day,
    As it is seyde yn the prophecye,
8 In the book of Jeremye.
    Herkenyth now þe tokenynge

I. Rain shall fall, bitter as gall,

    That þe firste day shal brynge :
    Fro heuyn shal a rayne falle,
12 Hit shal be byttyr as eny galle,

red as blood,

    Hytt shall be as red as any blod,
    Ouyr all þe worlle a grymly flod ;

and overwhelm the whole world,

    Hytt schalle ouergo wyth large mett
16 Alle that ys in erth I-sett :

and terrify children unborn.

    The chylderyn vn-born Aferd shall be
    Of thys tokenynge, as I telle the,
    And meue hem tyll our Syth
20 Ryth as þey speke myth.
    The secunde day ys stronge with alle :

II. The Stars shall fall from heaven.

    The sterrys shal fro heuyn falle,
    So dredfulle and so breyth
24 As the fyre off þe dondyr lyth.

QUINDECIM SIGNA ANTE DIEM IUDICIJ. 119

Men schall*e* say, "well*e*-away!
Thys ben the tokenys off domys day!"
They schall cry & syke sore,
28 And say, "lord, m*er*cy, thyn ore¹!"   [¹ MS. thynore]
The iij^{de} day ys off syche: III. The Sun
In erthe and in heuyn-ryche
The hye son thatt ys so bryth,
32 So fayr, and so full off lyth,
Hitt shall*e* be swarte as any pyche: shall turn black as pitch.
All*e* thatt shall be rewlyche.
Men schall*e* þen sone so
36 Att mydday hytt shall*e* swarte be;
All thatt ben on lyve
Schall*e* thys wordys dryve.
"Alas thatt we scholl*e* Abyde
40 To se þis sorowe in Eu*er*y syde!"
The iiij^{te} day ys swythe longe,   IV. Everything
W*ith* wepynge & wyth sorow Amonge:
All þat in erthe stonde   on earth shall turn into red blood
44 Schall to red blod wende;
They schall*e* drawe he*m* to þe grownde,
Ther schall*e* they dwelle butt no stownde,
To the see þey schall*e* for drede,   and flee to the sea.
48 Ryth as moyses the p*r*ophytt sayde,
Thatt the mone schall*e* rewly falle   The Moon shall fall from heaven.
And wynd outt of hys reche stalle.
The man schall*e* say to hys wyff
52 "Alas þatt we be nowe Alyve!"
The v^{te} day comyth swythe;   V. All beasts shall hold up their heads towards heaven.
For eu*er*y best þatt ys on lyve,
Toward heuyn her hedd schall holde.
56 For thatt wonþ*er* As y yowe tollde,
Mon schall*e* say, "lord, thyn ore   Men shall pray God mercy,
Off our sorowe & off our sore!"
Thys tellyth the p*r*ophecy
60 In þe booke of Jeromy.

and ask Christ to	Well*e* we schall*e* vndyrstonde
	Thatt cristyndom hatt vn*per*fonge.
[¹ Omitted, and inserted in Margin.] bring them to bliss.	"Thatt day, Ih*esus* to vs se
	64 As þou¹ vs bowtyst vppon a tre,
	Thatt we may com to þy blysse
	Lord, when þy will*e* ys!"
VI. The Trees shall turn upside down,	The vj day schall down Fall*e*
	68 The treys wit*h* þe croppys all*e*,
	And toward þe erthe the croppys schall*e* be.
	For fere the man schall*e* lese hys wyff,
and children shall die.	The wyff her chyld, þe chylld hys lyff;
	72 All*e* thatt leve schall lese here wytte;
	Wo they be thatt schall*e* a-byde hytte,
	Bettyr they were to be oute off lyve
	Than soche payne for to dryve.
VII. All castles shall fall down.' [² MS. *down*]	76 The vij day schall*e* fall down
	Chyrche and castell*e* and eue*r*y town²;
The hills shall be lowered and fill up the valleys,	All schall to-breke; and eue*r*y hyll*e*
	Shall*e* lowe, valeys For to Fyll*e*;
	80 The erthe schall*e* [be] shene and clene;
	In þis worll*e* all*e* schall*e* be evyn;
so that all the earth shall be even.	Than schall*e* þe worll*e* evyn be:
	Wo ys he þ*a*t thatt schall*e* se!
VIII. A day of dread.	84 The viij day ys a day off drede,
	Ryth as moyses þe p*r*ophytt seyde
The Sea will rise and flee,	Thatt the see woll ryse & fle,
	Thatt eue*r*y best aferd schall be;
	88 Than for drede hytt woll ryse & flowe
	Wi*th* wawys grete, & stormys towe:
and be driven up to the clouds by the wind.	Thorowe the strength off þe wynd
	Into the Welken hitt schall slynge;
All living will wish to be hid under the earth.	92 All thatt lenyth þatt day
	Wold fle away, but þey ne may;
	Vndyr erthe I-hydd they wold be
	Thatt Ih*esu* cryst scholl nott hem Ase.
	96 Then wolle the see wytdrawe,

QUINDECIM SIGNA ANTE DIEM IUDICIJ.

  And wend to hys owyn hawe.
  Godd of heuyn, þat best may,
  Haue mercy on vs vppon þatt day!
100 The ix day, wondyr hytt ys,   *IX. As the prophecy tells,*
  As the prophecy tellyth hytt I wys:
  Thatt all þynge schall speke þan,   *all things on earth shall speak*
  And cry in erthe aftyr þe steuyn off man, *with the voice of man and bemoan*
104 And be-mone hem self in owr syȝth   *themselves.*
  Ryth as þey speke myth.
  Lord Ihesu, thy myth þou fullfelle!
  We be sorry þatt we dede agayn þi wille
108 Or with towyth or with dede.
  Lord Ihesu! brenge vs oute of þis drede   *Jesu, bring us from this dread*
  Thatt we may com to rest!   *to rest, with Thee.*
  Ther bale ys most, & bote ys nexte.
112 The .x. day ys day of welaway   *X. A day of lamentation.*
  As gregory sayth, and Jeromy:
  Than schalle knele þe angelys bryth   *The Angels shall kneel before God.*
  Before þe face of godd allmyth.
116 Seynt peter, noþer his felow-redde,   *Peter and his companions*
  Dar nott speke A word for drede;   *shall not dare to speak.*
  They schalle se heuyn vngo,   *Heaven and earth shall move onwards (?)*
  And þe erthe schall Also,
120 They schalle schryke & crye lome
  For þe drede of þe grett dome.
  Develyn schall com oute off helle   *Devils shall come out of hell*
  As seynt Johan doyth vs tell,
124 They schalle kry, "lord, thyn ore   *and pray God to*
  Off our sorowe & of our sore!
  Lett vs to heuyn com!   *let them come back in to heaven.*
  Longe þou hast hytt vs be-nome
128 For our gylt, and our mysdede,
  And for our awyn wykkyd rede!"
  Thys ys a day of moche sorowe;
  A strongyr comyth on the morrowe.
132 The xi day comyth lyche,   *XI. Great storms*

QUINDECIM SIGNA ANTE DIEM IUDICIJ.

shall rage;
all rocks and stones shall clash together,
and all the world.

The Rainbow shall be twisted,

and the Devils shall run back to hell.

XII. This day is dreadful.

Angels shall fall

at God's feet for us.

Lord, be merciful!

XIII. Of this day,

no one can tell half the sorrow.

All the stones on earth

shall drive ı against one another

      W*ith* stronge stormys sykyrlyche,
      And all*e* the stonys moche & lyte
      Scholl*e* to-gedyr sore smyte ;
136 Alle the worll*e* schall*e* to-dryv*e* ;
      Wo be þey þatt ben on lyve !
      The rayn bowe Iwryyd schall*e* be,
      Grymlyche In sy3th for to see.
140 Than the deuelyn schall*e* swyde ren,
      And for fere to helle torn ;
      God will*e* say, " ther schull ye be,
      Ther schall ye wone & be war,"
144 God grownte so to be-tyde
      Thatt we may be on bettyr syde !
      The xij day ys dredfull*e* than,
      For than was neu*er* schappe of man
148 That woll*e* þatt god dyd hy*m* ryth
      Yff he dyrst, & most of myth.
      Angelys thatt hy*m* s*er*uyn all*e*
      Scholl for vs vppon kneys falle
152 To goddys feett for our syn ;
      And for the loue of all man kyn.
      Lord we be-seche the
      In þi m*er*cy for to be !
156 Dredfully comyth the xiij day
      To all þatt Abyde hytt may.
      Fro the begynnynge of Adamys com
      Tyll*e* the end of þe day of doome,
160 Ne myth no man in booke rede
      Half the sorow, noþ*er* half þe drede,
      That god schall*e* say than
      When he comyth down yn schappe of man,
164 For all*e* the stonys grett and smal*e*
      Thatt byth in erthe wi*th*outyn tale,
      All they schall*e* to-gedyr drynge,
      And eu*er*ychon to oþ*er* dynge ;
168 They schall ryse & grynd so

	Thatt þe fyr fro hem schalle go;	so that fire shall fly from them
	They schall bren also bryth	
	As þe fyr of þe dondyr lyth.	like lightning.
172	The xiiij day ys A day of sorowe;	XIV. Fire shall come in the morning and burn up every thing on earth till the evening.
	Stronge fyr schalle com on þe morow,	
	Ther schalle nothyng in þys worlle leve	
	Butt schalle bren to morów tyll eve.	
176	Thys passyth nott swythe sone;	
	On the morow ys þe day of doome.	
	The xv day comyth swythe:	XV. The Day of Doom. All men that have lived since Adam's time,
	For euery man þat was on lyve	
180	Fro Adamys tyme, the fyrst man,	
	Alle to the dome schalle com than,	
	Euery man of xxx^{ti} wynter olde,	every one made 30 years old, shall come
	All schall com þe dome to be-holde;	
184	Euery man schalle oþere mete	
	Att the mownte of olevett.	to Mount Olivet.
	Two angelys schall blowe her bemys;	Two angels shall blow their trumpets,
	The folke schall com alle attonys.	
188	Fulle sore than they may Agryse	
	Whan they shulle to þe dome aryse,	
	Two angelys schall com be-forne	two shall bring the scourges that beat Christ, and the Crown of Thorns
	With þe scorges, and with the crowne of thorn	
192	With drewry cher and sory mode	
	As hytt on hys hedd stode;	as it stood on His head,
	And the sper al so scharpe	with the spear,
	As hytt stod on hys hertt.	as it stood on His heart.
196	For no enuy, ne for no pryde,	(Longeùs, the soldier, did not pierce Christ from envy or pride, but
	Longeus hym stonge dorow þe syde:	
	Longeus then styll stode,	
	On hys fyngorys ran þe blod,	
200	He strokyd ther-with hys eyn ryth,	put Christ's blood on his eyes, and they became as clear as candle-light. 'Piteous Lord, forgive me, who pierced Thee, my guilt.')
	They be-coom as cler as candyllyȝth.	
	"Kynge and lord full of pyte,	
	Thys mys-gylt þou for-yeue me!	
204	I dyd hyt for non evyll dede,	

QUINDECIM SIGNA ANTE DIEM IUDICIJ.

<table>
<tr><td>

Angels shall bring the Cross and bloody nails.

Then Christ, sad, shall come,

and say, "Man, see what I suffered for thee! I was

crowned with thorns.
And thou lovedst to swear by My eyes, hair, and pains,

My five wounds,

teeth, tongue,

heart, lungs,

side, brains and head,
[1 ? *heved*]
nay, My soul.

Such shame thou didst me!

Thou wouldst not feed or help me.

What hast thou suffered for Me?"

Then comes Our Lady, weeping

tears of blood,

and saying,

"King and Lord, my sweet Son,
[2 *thee*]
grant me to-day my prayer.
Lose not Thy handiwork

</td><td>

208

212

216

220

224

228

232

236

240

</td><td>

No þer for no covetyse of mede."
Angelys schall brenge þe rode bryth,
With blody naylys precyous of syth.
Then comyth our lord with drewry mode,
Wyth armys I-spred all on blod :
" Man, now þe soth þou mayst I-se,
Whatt I sufferd her for the.
Thys passyon I sufferd her for þe :
I-cronyd I was with thornys of a tre ;
Thys was to the leff for to swere
Be my eyn & be myn here,
And be my paynys that wher stronge.
Man, hytt was þe fulle ryve
To swere be my wowndys fyve,
Be my tethe And my tonge,
Be my hertt and be my longe,
Hytt thowyth the fulle grett pryde
For to swere be my syde,
Be my brayne & be my hedd ; ¹
be my sowle I was ofte be-revyd.
Man, hytt was full grett dyspyte
So offte to make me edwyte !
Thou woldyst nott clothe me, ne fede,
Thou woldyst nott helpe me att my nede !
Man offte þou hast for-sworn me !
Man what sufferst þou for me ?"
Than comyth our lady hem be-fore—
In blyssyd tyme was she I-bore—
With terys rennynge alle on blodd,
Sore wepynge with drewry modd ;
" Fadyr, & son, and holygost,
Kynge and lord as þou wost,
My swete son, I praye de ²
My bone to day þou grawnt me !
Thy honde warke þat þou hast wrowyth,
My dere son, for-lese hem nowhte !

</td></tr>
</table>

QUINDECIM SIGNA ANTE DIEM IUDICIJ.

  Thou bowst hem wyth þy blodd   *bought with Thy blood.*
  And with þy flessch vppon þe rode ;
  My swete son, I pray the   *I pray Thee,*
244 For all mankynd þat I may be ;   *grant all men Thy bliss ;*
  Graw[n]te hem þy swete blysse,
  None of hem þatt þou ne mysse."   *miss none!"*
  "Modyr, thy wille I-fullfyllyd shall be,   *"Mother, thy will shall be done.*
248 Thy bone to day I grawnt hytt þe ;
  The goode y wille lese nowth,   *I will not lose the good.*
  My hondwerke that I haue wrowth.
  Thys þatt wallde nott serue me,   *Those who would not serve Me*
252 My blysse schalle they neuere se,
  Into payne they schalle wende,   *shall go to everlasting torment.*
  To haue [3] hytt euere withoutyn ende.   *[3 haue repeated in MS.]*
  My chyldryn þat haue seruyd me,   *My children, who have served Me,*
256 In my blysse they schall euere be ;
  Ye scholl com with me to heuyn   *shall come with Me to heaven."*
  With angelys songe and mery steuyn.
  And he clepyth hym be-fore,—
260 In blyssyd tyme wer they I-bore,—
  He spekyth to hem myldelyche,
  "Comyth with me to my kyngdome ryche."
  Lord we be-seche þe   *Lord, grant us to see Thy bliss when we die!*
264 Thy swete blysse þatt we mott se ;
  When we com to oure lyvys ende,
  Into thy blysse þat we mot wende,
  And grawnt vs thatt hytt so be !
268 Amen, Amen, lord, For charite !   *Amen!*

[For the meaning of l. 182, see Hampole's *Pricke of Conscience*, ed. Morris, 1863, p. 135, lls. 4983-90.
   Þan sal alle ryse in þe same eld þan
   Þat God had fully here als man . . . .
   Þan was he of threty yhere elde, and twa,
   And of thre monethes þar-with alswa ;
   In þat elde alle sal ryse at the last
   When þai here þe grete bemes blast.]

Who can not Wepe, com lerne of me.

(THE VIRGIN'S SONG OVER HER DEAD SON.)

[*MS. O. 9. 38, Trin. Coll. Cambridge. Written mostly as prose.*]

<small>A woman fair sat weeping</small>

Sodenly A-frayd, halfe wakynge halfe slepyng,
and gretly dysmayd, A woman sate wepyng,
With fauour in here face far passynge my reson,
4 And of here sore wepyng þis was þe encheson;

<small>over her dead son lying in her lap,</small>

Here sone yn here lappe layd, sche seyd, sleyn by treson:
yf wepyng myȝt rype be, hit semyd then yn seson.

<small>lamenting how Jesus was robbed of his life,</small>

Ihesus, so sche sobbed,
8 so here sone was bobbed
And of hys lyue robbed;

<small>saying, 'Who cannot weep, come learn of me.'</small>

Seynge thys wordys as y sey the,
"Who can not wepe, com lerne of me."

<small>"I cannot weep."</small>

12 y seyd y cowde not wepe, y was so hard hertyd.
Sche answerd me schortly with wordys þat smartyd,

<small>'Nature shall make thee,</small>

"Lo, nature schall meve þe; thow must be conuertyd,

<small>thy father is dead;</small>

thyn owne fadyr thys nyȝth ys dede:" thys schee twhertyd:

<small>my son is robbed of his life.'</small>

16 "Ihesus, so my sone ys bobbed,
and of hys lyue robbed.
ffor soth then y sobbed

Veryfyyng thys wordys, seyng to the,
20 Who can not wepe com lerne at me."

"Now, breke hert, y the praye ! thys cord lycth so rulye, *'Break, my heart! for my son so foully used.*
So betyn, so woundyd, Entretyd so fuly.
What wy3t may be-hold, and wepe not? none truly, *Who could see him and not weep?'*
24 to see my ded dyre sone bledynge, lo, thys newly !"
Euer stylle schee sobbed, *So still she sobbed how her son was slain.*
So here sone was bobbed
And of hys lyue robbed.
28 Newyng these wordys, as y sey the,
"Who can not wepe, com lerne at me."

On me sche cast here yee, and seyd, "see, man, thy brother !"
Sche kyste hym, and seyd, "swete, am y not thy modyr ?" *She kissed him;*
32 And swonynge schee fylle; ther hyt wold be no nothyr : *she swooned;*
y not whych more dedlye, the tone or the todyr.
yett sche reuyued, and sobbed *and reviving, she sobbed how her son was bobbed,*
how here sone was bobbed
36 & of hys lyue robbed.
"Who can not wepe," thys ys the lay, *and then vanished away.*
And with that wordys schee vanyschyd A-way.·.
ffinis.

The Death of Archbishop Scrope

(WHO WAS BEHEADED, 8 JUNE, 1405).

[*From MS. R. 4. 20, Trin. Coll. Cambridge, on a blank leaf at the end of Lydgate's Siege of Thebes.*]

Wise Bishop Scrope is dead,	Hay hay hay hay thynke oñ Whitsonmonday.	
	The bysshop Scrope that was so wyse	
	Nowe is he dede and lowe he lyse	hay
but by Mary's help he may rise to heaven.	To hevyns blys yhit may he ryse	
	4 Thurghe helpe of Marie that mylde may	
On the hill he took his death right willingly.	Wheñ he was broght vnto the hylle	
	He held hym̄ both mylde and stylle	hay
	He toke his deth with fulle gode wylle	
	8 As I haue herde fulle trewe men say	
His executioner knelt to him and asked his forgiveness.	He that shulde his dethe be	
	He kneled downe vppoñ his kne	hay
	Lord your deth forgyffe it me	
	12 Fulle hertly here to yowe I pray	
He granted it, asking for five strokes to send him to heaven.	Here I wylle the commende	
	yᵘ gyff me fyve strokys with thy hende	hay
	And theñ my wayes yᵘ latt me wende	
	16 To hevyns blys that lastys ay	

[Compare Hall's Chronicle, *Hen. IV.* fol. xxv (ed. 1550) W. A. W.]

EXTRACT FROM *HALLE* AS TO ARCHBISHOP SCROPE'S
DEATH. ED. 1543 ?(HY. ELLIS) FOL. XXV.

KYNG HENRY THE .IIII.

¶ THE SIXT YERE.

IN this yere the Earle of Northumber- The vi   The Earl of
lande, which bare styll a venemous   yere.   Northumberland
scorpion in his cankered heart, and coulde   conspired with
not desist to inuent and deuise waies and meanes howe
to be reuenged of kyng Henry and his fautours, began
secretely to communicate his interior imaginacions and
priuie thoughtes with Richard Scrop, Archebishop of   Archbishop
Yorke, brother to william lord Scrop, treasorer of   Scrope,
England, whome kyng Henry (as you have heard) beheaded at the towne of Bristow, and with Thomas   Earl Mowbray,
Mowberey, erle Marshal, sonne to Thomas duke of
Norffolke, for kyng Henries cause before banished
the realme of England, and with the lordes, Hast-
ynges, Fauconbridge, Bardolfe, and diverse other   and others, against
whiche he knewe to beare deadely hate and inward
grudge toward the kyng. After long consultacion   Henry,
had, it was finally concluded and determined amongest   and all agreed to
theym, that all they, their frendes and alies, with all
their power, should mete at Yorkeswold at a day   meet at Yorkes-
appointed, and that therle of Northumberland should   wold on a day
be chefetaine and supreme gouernour of the armie,   appointed.
which promised to bring with him a great number of
Scottes.

This sedicious conspiracye was not so secretly kept,
nor so closely cloked, but that the kyng therof had
knowledge, and was fully aduertised. wherfore to pre-
uent the time of their assembly, he, with suche power   But before this
as he could sodainly gather together, with all diligence   Henry marched
                                                        northwards,

marched toward the North parties, and vsed suche a celeritie in his iourney that he was thither come with all his hoste and power before the confederates hearde any inkelyng of his marchyng forward; and sodainly there wer apprehended the archebishop, the earle Marshall, sir Iohn Lampley, and sir Robart Plumpton. These personnes wer arrained, atteinted, and adiudged to die; and so on the Monday in Whytson weke all they withoute the Citie of Yorke were beheaded.

Here of necessitie I ought not, nor will not, forgeate how some foolishe and fantasticall personnes haue wrytten, howe erronius Ippocrites and sedicyous Asses haue endited, howe supersticious Fryers and malycious Monkes haue declared and diuulged—bothe contrary to goddes doctrine, the honoure of their prince, and common knowen veritie—that at the howre of the execucion of this Bishop (which of the Execucioner desired to haue fiue strokes in remembraunce of the fiue woundes of Christ) the kyng at the same tyme syttyng at diner had .v. strokes in his necke by a person inuisible, & was incontinently striken with a leprey; which is a manifest lye, as you shall after plainely perceiue.

What shall a man say of suche writers whiche toke upon them to knowe the secretes of Goddes iudgement? what shall men thinke of suche beastly personnes, whiche, regardyng not their bounden dutie and obeisance to their prynce & souerain Lorde, enuied the punishment of traiters and torment of offenders. But what shall all men coniecture of suche whyche, fauorynge theyr owne worldly dignitie, their owne priuat auctorite, their owne peculiar profit, wyl thus iuggle, raile, and imagine fantasies agaynst their soueraigne lorde and Prince, and put them in memorye as a miracle to his dyshonor and perpetuall infamy: well let wyse men iudge what I haue said.

GLOSSARY.

Abie, p. 26, l. 130; p. 96, l. 22, pay for, atone for; A.S. *abicgan.*
Abowe, p. 97, l. 69, bow, bend, humble.
Adwiten, p. 70, l. 396, blame, accuse; A.S. *edwítan.*
Aȝenseid, p. 94, l. 100, denied.
Aggregidist, p. 52, l. 346, *aggreger*, to aggravate. Cotgrave.
Agryse, p. 123, l. 188, A.S. *agrysan*, to fear.
Among, p. 81, l. 59, at intervals, 'amonge, or sum tyme, *interdum, quandoque.*' P. Parv.
Apeele, p. 71, l. 433, Fr. *appeler*, to accuse, appeach, or charge with. Cot.
Aslake, p. 80, l. 47, A.S. *aslacian*, slacken, dissolve.
Aslope, p. 54, l. 427, aside.
Asswage, p. 79, l. 10, quiet down; Fr. *assouvager*, to assuage, quiet, still, pacifie. Cot.
Attir, p. 24, l. 62, poisonous.
Auauntage, at his, p. 81, l. 70, in his power, control.
Awaite, p. 76, l. 593, ? watch.

Balke, p. 92, l. 47, baulk, a mess of his life.

Beerde, p. 13, l. 50, woman, maiden.
Beete, p. 12, l. 11, A.S. *gebétan*, to amend, atone for.
Bemys, p. 123, l. 186, trumpets; A.S. *béme.*
Bigoon, p.16, l. 40, overwhelmed; A.S. *begán*, to go over.
Bihatid, p. 82, l. 24, thoroughly hated.
Bihiȝt, p. 19, l. 52, promised; A.S. *beháten.*
Bikir, p. 46, l. 15, strife.
Binam, p. 92, l. 34, took away from; A.S. *benám.*
Bitake, p. 20, l. 74, commit; A.S. *betœcan.*
Bleere, p. 60, l. 78, mock, scorn; 'I gyue him the best counsayle I can, and the knaue *bleareth* his tonge at me, *tirer la langue.*' Palsgrave.
Blynne, p. 97, l. 66, cease.
Blyue, p. 46, l. 177; p. 96, l. 30, quickly.
Bobbed, p. 126, l. 8, beaten; 'bobet on the heed, *coup de poing.*' Palsgrave.
Boone, p. 6, l. 21, prayer; A.S. *ben.*

Bote, p. 11, l. 104, remedy; A.S. *bót*.
Boteles, p. 108, l. 42, remediless.
Breme, p. 102, l. 31, ?not A.S. *breme*, glorious, but '*brym* or fers. *Ferus, ferox.*' Pr. Parv.
Broode, p. 37, l. 77, abroad, about.

Careful, p. 16, l. 39, full of care and trouble.
Cesoun, p. 42, l. 28, ?seizin, possession, or 'take a cesoun,' stay a season or time.
Chesoun, p. 42, l. 32, cause, reason; O.Fr. *achaison*, occasion.
Clene, p. 1, l. 7, pure; 'Clene, *mundus, purus.*' Pr. Parv.
Clennesse, p. 64, l. 197, purity.
Clinge, p. 85, l. 68; p. 89, l. 20, A.S. *clingan*, to wither, cling, or shrink up.
Conclude, p. 77, l. 605, shut up.
Contrarie, p. 37, l. 87, go contrary to.
Coorde, p. 38, l. 111, accord, agree.
Coost, p. 34, l. 63, Fr. *costé*, a coast or quarter. Cotgrave.
Countirtaile, p. 71, l. 416, Fr. *contretaille*, the one part of a tallie, or score, alreadie mafked, or notched. Cotgrave.
Croppys, p. 120, l. 68, tops; A.S. *crop*, top, bunch, berry.
Cunne, p. 114, l. 15, A.S. *cunnan*, to know.
Cus, p. 12, l. 22, kiss; A.S. *cus, cyss*.

Daswen, p. 68, l. 338, become dazed or dim; Du. *duyster*, dim.
Defie, p. 95, l. 6, fear for?
Delice, p. 78, l. 633; Delijs, p. 42, l. 43, Fr. *delices*, delights, pleasures.
Dere, p. 110, l. 67, injure; A.S. *derian*.
Derworþiest, p. 52, l. 352, A.S. *deorwurđe*, precious, of great value.
Diffence, p. 60, l. 63, Fr. *defense*, answer, argument.
Discure, p. 63, l. 165, discover.
Dispence, p. 63, l. 157, gain, reward?
Disceyuable, p. 86, l. 7, deceitful.
Disperage, p. 74, l. 508, incongruity; O.Fr. *desparager*, to offer vnto, or impose on, a man vnfit, or unworthie conditions. Cot.
Dondyr, p. 118, l. 24, thunder.
Drewis, p. 60, l. 66 ? draughts.
Drynge, p. 122, l. 166, A.S. *þringan*, throng, rush.
Dwynne, p. 27, l. 176, dwindle; A.S. *dwinan*, to pine, fade, waste away.

Edwyte, p. 124, l. 226, reproach, twitting; A.S. *edwíte*, reproach, disgrace, contumely.
Encheson, p. 10, l. 75, occasion; O. French, *achaison*.
Ensure, p. 18, l. 9, cock sure.
Entensioun, p. 21, l. 92, ? excuse, or mind.
Eruest, p. 69, l. 350, harvest; A.S. *hærfest*.

Faite, p. 77, l. 595, ?deceive; O.Fr. '*faiteus*, criminel, coupable.'
Fare, p. 95, l. 13, goings on, ways, life.
Fawe, p. 96, l. 28, fain, glad.
Felle, p. 25, l. 92, ? fail, or fell.
Fen, p. 26, l. 121, mire, mud.
Fere, p. 38, l. 111, company; *in fere*, together.
Fere, p. 86, l. 16, companion, person.
Filist, p. 114, l. 3, defilest.
Flaite, p. 75, l. 532, Du. *vleyden*, to flatter, to sooth, or to entice with faire [words]. Hexham.

Fleme, p. 18, l. 17, banish; A.S. *flyman*.

Florische, p. 89, l. 18, ornament, deck.

Foisoun, p. 43, l. 64, Fr. *foison*, plentie, great fullnesse. Cot.

Fondid, p. 8, l. 23, tried; A.S. *fandian*, to try.

Foondi, p. 95, l. 13, try.

Foonued, p. 96, l. 33, foolish?

For, p. 19, l. 35, 40, because.

Forbeere, p. 60, l. 76, restrain.

Forclonge, p. 18, l. 31, A.S. *clingan*, to wither, pine, or shrink up; *forclungen*, shrunk.

Forlete, p. 30, l. 250, A.S. *forlætan*, to let go.

Forþi, p. 24, l. 89, for that reason.

Foulden, p. 73, l. 485, ?fold, bend.

Frame, p. 44, l. 97, ? A.S. *freme*, profit, advantage.

Frauȝte, p. 76, l. 590, freight, load.

Frike, p. 23, l. 26, glad, joyful; A.S. *frician*, to dance, frisk.

Gesoun, p. 64, l. 206, ? Fr. *gesse*, a common sinke or sewer; a gutter for the voiding of ordure. Cotgr. Not. E. *geason*, rare, strange.

Gist, p. 93, l. 63, show.

Glewe, p. 29, l. 236, A.S *gleow*, joy, mirth, glee.

Grame, p. 63, l. 168, A.S. *grama*, anger, rage, wrath.

Greede, p. 14, l. 73, greet, moan; A.S. *grætan*, to weep, cry out.

Gril, p. 83, l. 12, sharp, unkind; O.N. *grila*. H. Coleridge.

Hadde-y-wist, p. 73, l. 497, had-I-known (what would have happened), after-regret.

Happe, p. 89, l. 26, wrap over, cover for defence; Isl. *hypia*, Jamieson.

Harewide, p. 53, l. 385, tore open.

Hawe, p. 121, l. 97, A.S. *hæh*, hole, den.

He, p. 59, l. 39, they.

Hende, p. 7, l. 25, gentle.

Hildande, p. 23, l. 55, beholden.

Hirde, p. 17, l. 52, A.S. *hirde*, a shepherd.

Ho, p. 14, l. 71, halt, stop.

Homeli, p. 63, l. 163, familiar.

Hore, p. 83, l. 13, hoar, hoariness.

Hote, p. 41, l. 15, be called; A.S. *hátan*.

Ilke, p. 23, l. 54, every.

Insiȝt, p. 66, l. 250; p. 69, l. 339, 'insyght, *inspexio, circumspeccio*.' Promptorium.

Kinde, p. 20, l. 59, nature.

Kiþe, p. 11, l. 92, show; A.S. *cyðan*, to make known, declare, show.

Kynde, p. 9, l. 53, nature; A.S. *ge-cynd*.

Kyndeli, p. 8, l. 19, natural; A.S. *ge-cyndelic*.

Lappid, p. 3, l. 50, wrapped; 'Lappyn, or whappyn yn cloþys (happyn to-gedyr, wrap togeder in clothes). *Involvo*.' P. Parv.

Lauȝt, p. 30, l. 249; p. 76, l. 586, caught, taken; A.S. *læccan*, to seize.

Leeme, p. 52, l. 335, A.S. *leoma*, light, flame.

Leepis, p. 47, l. 181; p. 72, l. 451, A.S. *leap*, a basket, hamper.

Leere, p. 8, l. 5, teach; A.S. *læran*.

Lees, p. 16, l. 45, lies.

Leit, p. 48, l. 226; Leite, p. 52, l. 355, lightning; A.S. *lihting*.

Lende, p. 23, l. 41, lent; A.S. *lened*.

Lent, p. 105, l. 26, put away?; ? A.S. *lengde*, put off, *perf.* of *lengian*.

Lete, p. 28, l. 186, leave, cease; A.S. *lætan*, let go.
Lewide, p. 67, l. 303, lay, ignorant.
Leye, p. 95, l. 2, field after the crop is cut, *clover ley*, &c.; ? not A.S. *lagu*, a district in which a certain law was in force.
Likerose, p. 20, l. 55, lecherous.
Likid, p. 8, l. 16, pleased.
Liking, p. 3, l. 50, pleasant.
Likinge, p. 92, l. 49; p. 93, l. 77, 81, lust.
Likingly, p. 91, l. 20, pleasantly.
List, p. 4, l. 3; A.S. *list*, wisdom, science, power, faculty; *lyst*, desire, love, admiration.
Lome, p. 121, l. 120, frequently; A.S. *gelóme*.

Maistrie, p. 20, l. 80, mastery, (see p. 33, l. 58,) ? not tricks.
Mammillis, p. 1, l. 5, breasts, paps; Pappe, *Mamilla*. P. Parv.
Maugre, p. 65, l. 215, reviling, railing; Fr. *maugréer*, to curse, reuile extreamly, raile on despightfully.
Mawmetis, p. 45, l. 118, idols.
Medele, p. 20, l. 86, mingle.
Meene, p. 1, l. 4, remember; A.S. *mœnan*.
Meete, p. 1, l. 6, food.
Melle, p. 53, l. 387, meddle.
Mengid, p. 59, l. 51, A.S. *mengian*, mix, mingle.
Mett, p. 118, l. 15, measure; A.S. *mete*.
Mydmore, p. 83, l. 17, midmorning.
Mynde, p. 9, l. 25, ? mention, or A.S. *myne*, memory.
Mynne, p. 24, l. 78, remember.
Myscheue, p. 90, l. 46, come to grief.
Mystire, p. 76, l. 572, need; Fr. *mestier*, need, lacke, necessitie, want. Cotgrave.

Nempne, p. 6, l. 7, name; A.S. *nemnan*.
Newyng, p. 127, l. 28, renewing, repeating.
Nuyʒed, p. 106, l. 13, annoyed, troubled.
Nyce, p. 53, l. 390, Fr. *niais*, a simple, witlesse, and vnexperienced gull. *Nice*, lither, lazie, sloathfull, dull, simple. Cot.
Nym, p. 53, l. 371, take; A.S. *niman*, to take.

Of, p. 98, l. 101, from.
Ore, p. 119, l. 57, mercy.
Ouerhope, p. 68, l. 331, too much confidence, sanguineness.

Paieth, p. 24, l. 58, pleases.
Pay, p. 14, l. 80, satisfaction, pleasure; *payé*, satisfied, contented. Cotgrave.
Pilis, p. 64, l. 182, peels, holds, castles.
Piʒt, p. 3, l. 61, pitched; p. 4, l. 13; p. 94, l. 90, placed; p. 12, l. 16, put, dressed.
Pooste, p. 43, l. 79, power.
Port, p. 93, l. 85, mien.
Prest, p. 45, l. 116, quickly.
Prouʒ, p. 50, l. 288, advantage, profit; Fr. *prou*.
Pure, p. 18, l. 11, purify.
Pursue, p. 68, l. 328, follow, strive.
Put, p. 73, l. 475, throw, casting.

Queed, p. 6, l. 18, wicked one, devil; Dutch, *quaad*.
Qwart, p. 23, l. 2, of good heart or cheer; O.Fr. *quor*, courage.
Qweme, p. 18, l. 15, A.S. *cweman*, to please.

Race, p. 48, l. 238, A.S. *ræs*, rush, attack; cp. mill*race*.

GLOSSARY.

Raþer, p. 88, l. 16, earlier, sooner.
Raþir, p. 86, l. 9, preferable.
Releef, p. 47, l. 181, leavings.
Remewe, p. 20, l. 69, remove.
Rere, p. 70, l. 379, late. *Rere* suppers are complained of in Waddington (b. 1300), Robert of Brunne, 1303, A.D., and many other writers.
Rereage, p. 73, l. 483, arrears.
Reueþ, p. 30, l. 257, bereaves, takes away.
Riʒt, p. 46, l. 170, upright, straight.
Rijfe, p. 92, l. 29, much; Du. *rijf*, rife, abundant.
Romage, p. 93, l. 60, roaming.
Rouʒte, p. 36, l. 38, recked; A.S. *róhte*.
Rowne, p. 63, l. 163, whisper.
Ruli, p. 10, l. 68, grievous; p. 89, l. 27, sad, mournful; A.S. *hreów*, grief, pénitence; *hreówlic*, cruel, mournful.
Ryve, p. 124, l. 217 (see *rijfe*), customary, frequent.

Sadli, p. 8, l. 7, fixedly.
Sale, p. 57, l. 502; Fr. *salle*, hall.
Saugʒte, p. 76, l. 592, A.S. *saht*, reconciled.
Sauʒten, p. 108, l. 38, reconcile; A.S. *sehtian*. Note the change to *soften* in the later text, p. 109.
Schende, p. 11, l. 118, shame, disgrace, ruin; A.S. *sceond*, shame, disgrace.
Schendiþ, p. 53, l. 374, A.S. *scendan*, to confound, shame, reproach, revile.
Schille, p. 65, l. 232; schylle and sharpe, *acutus, sonorus.*
Schowr, p. 44, l. 96, A.S. *scúr*, battle, fight.
Sconfitith, p. 46, l. 154, discomfits.

Scryue, p. 58, l. 2, describe.
Secke, p. 76, l. 589, sack, bag.
See, p. 13, l. 54, seat.
Seelde, p. 41, l. 6, seldom.
Seete, p. 37, l. 89, set.
Sege, p. 2, l. 35, seat; Fr. *siège*.
Seruile, p. 104, l. 15, of service, of business.
Sijkè, p. 78, l. 634, sickness; Du. *zieck*, sick.
Sikir, p. 33, l. 50, certain, sure.
Skile, p. 9, l. 33, reason; O.N. *skil*.
Slake, p. 11, l. 112, become slack, cease.
Slidir, p. 49, l. 269, slydyr (or swypyr as a wey). *Lubricus*, P. Parv.
Smerte, p. 93, l. 67, smart, pain, prick.
Soote, p. 29, l. 248, sweet one.
Spaynel, p. 91, l. 4, spaniel; Fr. *espagneul*, a Spaniell. Cot.
Spousebriche, p. 47, l. 188, adultery.
Spurne, p. 43, l. 76, A.S. *spurnan*, to strike with the heel; p. 91, l. 11, spurned.
Spute, p. 46, l. 164, dispute.
Stabilte, p. 26, l. 144, fixedness, firmness.
Stie, p. 90, l. 48, ascend.
Stiʒ, p. 55, l. 460, ascended; AS. *stígan*, to ascend, rise.
Stintith, p. 116, l. 62, stoppeth.
Sue, p. 20, l. 68, follow.
Suffraunce, p. 33, l. 50, Fr. *souffrance*, sufferance, forbearance, patience, abiding.
Sunge, p. 110, l. 73, sin; A.S. *syngian*.
Superflue, p. 89, l. 30, superfluous.
Swarte, p. 119, l. 33, dark, black (swarthy).
Swing, p. 28, l. 203, A.S. *swingan*, to whip, scourge.

GLOSSARY.

Swiþe, p. 69, l. 348, quickly.
Swyde, p. 122, l. 140, quickly.
Swynk, p. 89, l. 32, A.S. *swinc*, labour, *geswinc*, affliction, torment.

Temynge, p. 4, l. 20, childbirth; A.S. *teám*, offspring; *teámian*, *téman*, to propagate, beget.
Tende, p. 69, l. 369; tenden, p. 41, l. 6, attend.
Tene, p. 24, l. 71, A.S. *teóna*, injury, wrong.
Þat þat, p. 51, l. 310, that which.
Þee, p. 63, l. 176, thrive.
Þertille, p. 9, l. 37, thereto, in addition.
Þirle, p. 26, l. 147, pierce; A.S. *þirlian*.
Þole, p. 23, l. 27, A.S. *þolian*, suffer.
Þrong, p. 13, l. 27, driven, forced; A.S. *þringan*, to press, crowd.
Þrouȝ, p. 13, l. 32, A.S. *þruh*, a chest, coffin, sepulchre, grave.
Tille, p. 27, l. 168, to.
Toberste, p. 30, l. 251, burst all to pieces.
Tobreke, p. 29, l. 247, break to pieces.
Torent, p. 20, l. 82, rent to pieces.
Towe, p. 120, l. 29, tough, harsh; A.S. *tóh*.
Towyth, p. 121, l. 108, thought.
Twhertyd, p. 126, l. 15, retorted? A.S. *hweorfan*, to turn.
Twynne, p. 23, l. 37, separate.
Tyne, p. 25, l. 103, A.S. *tynan*, to hedge in, enclose, shut, close.

Uertu, p. 67, l. 300, power, strength.

Vertu, p. 72, l. 455, power, strength.
Vncele, p. 106, l. 21, unhappiness.
Vndirfonge, p. 69, l. 367, receive, take; A.S. *underfangan*, undertake, receive.
Vndirnome, p. 50, l. 289, ? tookest up or under, objectedst to; A.S. *underniman*, to undertake, comprehend.
Vngo, p. 121, l. 118, ? *vn* for *um*, round; A.S. *ymbgan*, go round.
Vndren, p. 84, l. 25, A.S. *undern*, the third hour, 9 a.m., extending also to noon.
Vnleueful, p. 110, l. 74, unlawful.
Vnneþe, p. 70, l. 373, A.S. *unéðelíce*, uneasily, with difficulty, scarcely, hardly.
Vnourne, p. 71, l. 404, A.S. *vnórnlic*, old, worn.
Vnsauȝte, p. 108, l. 37, unfriendly; A.S. *seht*, friendship, peace; *unseht*, want of friendship, enmity. Note the *unsoft* of the later text, p. 109.
Vnschent, p. 106, l. 6, unpunished.
Vnskilfully, p. 112, l. 90, unreasonably; *see* skil.
Vnsperid, p. 41, l. 15, set free, unlocked; 'speryn, or schettyn, *claudo*; speryn and schette wythe lokkys. Sero, obsero.' Pr. Parv.

Waitist, p. 50, l. 288, plannest.
Wake, p. 32, l. 8.; p. 99, l. 141, watch; A.S. *wæcan*.
Wan, p. 13, l. 41, wonnst, wentest.
Waterless, p. 20, l. 53, without water.
Wedde, p. 10, l. 60, pledge; A.S. *wed*.
Wede, p. 12, l. 18, garment; A.S. *wǽd*.
Welkid, p. 24, l. 68, faded, turned white; A.S. *wealcere*, a fuller, a whitener of cloths.
Wem, p. 83, l. 13, spot, A.S. *wem*.
Wente, p. 9, l. 51, gone.
Were, p. 106, 107, l. 2, danger;

A.S. *wér*, a fine for slaying a man; p. 116, l. 87, doubt?
Weuere, p. 77, l. 603, weaver, contriver, schemer.
White, p. 72, l. 450, quick, active; same as
Wiʒte, p. 63, l. 150; Sw. *vig*, active; '*wyte*, or delyvyr, or swyfte, Agilis, velox.' Pr. Parv.
Wiʒtli, p. 13, l. 41, swiftly, or powerfully.
Wijs, p. 98, l. 94, teach.
Wis, p. 11, l. 115; Wisse, p. 14, l. 68; A.S. *wissian*, to instruct, guide, govern.
Wite, p. 34, l. 67; p. 99, l. 4, know; A.S. *witan*.
Wiyte, p. 35, l. 8, 16, &c., blame, reproach, impute, ascribe to; A.S. *witan, witian*.
Wone, p. 11, l. 120, dwell; A.S. *wunian*.
Woniynge, p. 28, l. 199, dwelling.

Woost, p. 39, l. 35, knowest.
Worschipide, p. 53, l. 401, honoured.
Wreche, p. 16, l. 35, vengeance; A.S. *wræc*.

ʒeere, p. 65, l. 244; p. 67, l. 286, ? A.S. *geare*, certainly.
ʒeme, p. 52, l. 340; A.S. *giman*, govern, take care of.
ʒernynge, p. 28, l. 197, yearning, desire.
ʒore, p. 92, l. 35, formerly.
Yflet, p. 92, l. 37, fled, gone.
Yhit, p. 128, l. 3, yet.
Yloore, p. 79, l. 5, lost; A.S. *loren*.
Ymet, p. 81, l. 74, dreamt; A.S. *mætod*.
Ynne, p. 69, l. 359, ? bring in, not let in; A.S. *innan*, to go in, enter.
Ynow, p. 76, l. 567, enough.

NOTES.

P. 58. *Mirror of the Periods of Man's Life*. "The auncient sages by curious notes haue found out, that certaine yeeres in mans life be very perilous. These they name climactericall or stayrie yeares, for then they saw great alterations. Now a climactericall yeare is euery seauenth yeare . . Hence is it that in the seauenth !yeere children doe cast and renew their teeth. In the fourteenth yeere proceedeth the strippling age. In the one and twentieth, youth. And when a man hath past seauen times seauen years, to weet, nine and fortie yeares, he is a ripe and perfect man. Also, when he attaineth to ten times seauen yeeres, that is, to the age of threescore and ten, his strength and chiefest vertue beginnes to fall away." W. Vaughan, Natural and Artificial Directions for Health, 1602, pp. 47-8.

P. 128. Archbishop Scrope's Death. See the Latin Poem on this in Mr. Thomas Wright's "Political Songs," v. 2, p. 114-18.

INDEX OF FIRST LINES.

	Page
As y gan wandre in my walkinge	83
Bi a forest as y gan walke	95
Bothe ȝonge & oolde, wheþir ȝe be	32
Erþe out of erþe is wondirly wrouȝt	88
Euery man schulde teche þis lore	104
From þe tyme þat we were born	79
Hay, hay, hay, hay! thynke on Whitsonmonday	128
Heil be þou, marie, cristis moder dere	6
Heil be þou, marie, þe modir of crist	4
How mankinde dooþ bigynne. (The Mirror.)	58
If þou wole be weel with god. (A prose piece.)	40
Ihesu, lord, þat madist me. (Richard de Castre's Prayer.)	15
Ihesu, þi swetnes, who-so myȝte it se	8
Ihesus þat sprong of iesse roote	12
In a noon tijd of a somers day	91
In my ȝonge age ful wielde y was	35
In þee, god fadir, I bileeue	101
I warne vche leod þat lieuþ in londe (From the Vernon MS.)	106
I warne eche lijf þat lieuþ in lond	107

INDEX OF FIRST LINES.

	Page
Kyng of grace, & ful of pyte	118
Loue is lijf þat lastiþ ay	22
Man, among þi myrþis haue in mynde	114
Sodenly a-frayd, halfe wakynge, halfe slepyng	126
Surge, mea sponsa; swete in siȝt	1
There is no creature but oon	18
Whanne marye was greet with gabriel. (þe Deuelis Perlament)	41
Whi is þis world biloued þat fals is & veyn	86

The manufacturer's authorised representative in the EU for product safety is Oxford University Press España S.A. of El Parque Empresarial San Fernando de Henares, Avenida de Castilla, 2 - 28830 Madrid (www.oup.es/en or product.safety@oup.com). OUP España S.A. also acts as importer into Spain of products made by the manufacturer.
Printed and bound by CPI Group (UK) Ltd, Croydon, CR0 4YY

20/03/2026

02075337-0018